Messages from

Maitreya the Christ

One Hundred Forty Messages

Share Interna
London ◆ Amste

◆

The painting reproduced on the cover, painted by Benjamin Creme in 1974, represents 'The Flaming Diamond', the Greater Rod of Initiation, used at the third and higher Initiations by Sanat Kumara, the Lord of the World, on Shamballa. Charged at each World Cycle from the Central Spiritual Sun, it focusses Electrical Fire through the centres of the Initiate. There is a 'Lesser Rod' used by the Christ at the first two Initiations.

FOREWORD

Knowingly or not, the world stands ready to recognise the Christ. His long-awaited and hoped-for reappearance is now an accomplished fact.

On July 19, 1977, the Christ, Maitreya, the World Teacher, Head of our Spiritual Hierarchy, emerged from His ancient retreat and is now in the modern world. With His Disciples, the Masters of Wisdom, He will inaugurate the New Age of Synthesis and Brotherhood.

Benjamin Creme, British artist and esotericist, explains: "Early in September, 1977, I was taken before Maitreya Who asked if I would take, publicly, communications from Him which, since 1974, I had received in the privacy of the group with which I work. I said I would try, do my best. On September 6, 1977, the first public Message was given at Friends House, Euston Road, London, experimentally, to find out how I stood up to this kind of mental overshadowing and spiritual telepathy in public, a very different thing from the privacy of one's own group.

"The Messages are relayed by me to the audience. No trance or mediumship is involved, and the voice is mine, strengthened in power and altered in pitch by the overshadowing energy of Maitreya. They are transmitted simultaneously on all the astral and mental planes, while I supply the basic etheric-physical vibration for this to take place. From these subtle levels, the Messages impress the minds and hearts of countless people who are gradually made aware of the thoughts and the Presence of the Christ. A great thought-form is being built on the inner planes, embodying the fact of the Christ's Presence. This thought-form is then tuned into by the sensitives, clairvoyants and mediums of the world who, from now on, will increasingly bring in (in more or less distorted form)

1

the information of the Christ's return. He releases in this way fragments of His Teaching, to prepare the climate of hope and expectancy which will ensure His being accepted and followed, quickly and gladly.

"It is an enormous and embarrassing claim to have to make that the Christ is giving messages through oneself. But if people can rid their minds of the idea of the Christ as some sort of spirit, sitting in 'heaven' at God's right hand; if they can begin to see Him as indeed He is, a real and living man (albeit a Divine Man) who has never left the world; who descended, in 1977, not from 'heaven' but from His ancient retreat in the Himalayas, to complete the task He began in Palestine; as a great Master, an Adept and Yogi; as the chief actor in a Gospel Story which is essentially true, but much simpler than hitherto presented — if people can accept that possibility, then the claim to receive telepathic communications from such a closer and more knowable Being is also, perhaps, more acceptable. In any case, I leave it to a study of the quality of the Messages themselves to convince or otherwise. For many people, the energies which flow during the overshadowing convince. Many who come to the meetings at which these Messages are given are clairvoyant in various degrees, and their visions of the overshadowing as it takes place is for them the most convincing evidence of all."

The previous statement is extracted from the preface to *The Reappearance of the Christ and the Masters of Wisdom* by Benjamin Creme (Tara Press, 1980).

Through these communications, Maitreya, the Christ, suggests the lines that social change must take. He gives hints on how to recognise Him and urges His listeners to make known the fact of His Presence. He evokes also the desire to share and to serve humanity and Himself.

It is interesting to note how He returns to His themes again and again, presenting them differently and with growing emphasis. It is interesting, too, to see how every tenth Message (Nos. 10, 20, 30, and so on) stands out from the others; how in these He describes Himself in abstract terms as the embodiment of Divine Qualities rather than as the simple man, the brother and friend of humanity, which He is at pains to emphasise elsewhere.

It is recommended that readers take one Message at a time and read it aloud. In this way the rhythmic (mantric) quality of each Message can be better felt.

It is almost impossible to say these Messages aloud, with attention, without invoking the Christ's energy, His heart response. They are apparently simple, sent from heart to heart, but work on various levels and should be meditated upon for their full meaning to come through. Some people find it best to select one Message daily and meditate on that.

Many, singly and in groups, use in their meditations the tapes from which these Messages are transcribed. The Christ's energies, magnetised onto the tape as the Message is given, are released again at each replaying, thus enhancing the quality of the meditation.

BENJAMIN CREME

Message No. 1

September 6, 1977

My dear friends, it will not be long until you see My face.
When that time comes I shall take your hands in mine and
lead you to Him Whom we serve together.

My Manifestation is complete and accomplished.
I am, verily, in the world.

Soon you shall know Me, perhaps follow Me and love
Me.
My Love flows ever through you all.
And that Love, which I hold for all mankind, has brought
Me here.

My brothers and sisters, My Return to the world is a
signal that the New Age, as you call it, has commenced.

In this coming time, I shall show you beauties and
wonders beyond your imaginings, but which are your
birthright as sons of God.

My children, My friends, I have come more quickly,
perhaps, than you expected.
But there is much to do, much that needs changing in the
world.
Many hunger and die, many suffer needlessly.

I come to change all that; to show you the way forward
— into a simpler, saner, happier life — together. No
longer man against man, nation against nation, but
together, as brothers, shall we go forth into the New
Country.
And those who are ready shall see the Father's face.

4

May the Divine Love and Light and Power of the One
God be now manifest within your hearts and minds.
May this Light and Love and Power lead you to seek
That which dwells always in your heart's centre.
Find That, and make It manifest.

Message No. 2

September 15, 1977

Good evening, My dear friends.
I have taken, again, this opportunity to speak to you, and
to establish firmly in your minds the reasons for My
Return.

There are many reasons why I should descend and appear
once more among you. Chiefly they are as follows:

My Brothers, the Masters of Wisdom, are scheduled to
make Their group Return to the everyday world.
As Their Leader, I, as one of Them, do likewise.
Many there are throughout the world who call Me, beg
for My Return. I answer their pleas.
Many more are hungry and perish needlessly, for want of
the food which lies rotting in the storehouses of the world.
Many need My help in other ways: as Teacher, Protector;
as Friend and Guide.
It is as all of these I come.

To lead men, if they will accept Me, into the New Time,
the New Country, the glorious future which awaits
humanity in this coming Age;
for all of this I come.

I come, too, to show you the way to God, back to your
Source; to show you that the Way to God is a simple path
which all men can tread; to lead you upwards, into the
light of that New Truth which is the Revelation that I
bring.
For all of this I come.

6

Let Me take you by the hand and lead you into that beckoning country, to show you the marvels, the glories of God, which are yours to behold.

The vanguard of My Masters of Wisdom are now among you.
Soon you will know Them.
Help Them in Their work.
Know, too, that They are building the New Age, through you.
Let Them lead and guide, show you the way; and in doing this, you will have served your brothers and sisters well.

Take heart, My friends.
All will be well.
All manner of things will be well.

Good night, My dear friends.

May the Divine Light and Love and Power of the One God be now manifest within your hearts and minds.
May this manifestation lead you to seek That which dwells ever within you.
Find That, and know God.

Message No. 3

September 22, 1977

Good evening, My dear friends.

I am happy to be able to speak to you once more, and to
tell you that I come to take you with Me into the New
Country — the Country of Love, the Country of Trust, of
Beauty and Freedom.

I shall take you there if you can follow Me, accept Me,
let Me lead and guide.
And, if this be so, together we shall build a New World:

A world in which men can live without fear, without
mistrust, without division; sharing together the Earth's
bounty, knowing together the bliss of union with our
Source.

All this can be yours.
You have only to take the first steps and I may lead.

Allow Me to help you.
Allow Me to show you the way — forward, into a
simpler life where no man lacks; where no two days are
alike; where the joy of Brotherhood manifests through all
men.

Mine is the task to lead and guide, but you, willingly,
must follow.
Otherwise, I can do nothing. My hands are tied by Law.

The decision rests with mankind.

May the Divine Light and Love and Power of the One
God be now manifest within your hearts and minds.
May this manifestation lead you to seek and to find That
which dwells ever within you.
Identify with That and know God.

Message No. 4

September 29, 1977

My dear friends, I am pleased indeed to be able to speak to you once more in this fashion.

Many await My Coming with reverence and also with some fear.
This is inevitable.

My Coming will mean the end of the old order of things.
All that is useless, no longer serving the purposes of man, can now be discarded.

This will cause many to grieve but so it must be.

My friends, My children, I am here to show you that there exists for man a most marvellous future.
Decked in all the colours of the rainbow, glowing with the Light of God, man, one day, will stand upright in his divinity.
This I promise you.

I am a simple Man, and simply I make My Appeal to you:
Trust Me, follow Me, let Me take you into the future time, on the basis of Love,
on the basis of Sharing,
on the basis of Brotherhood.

Let Me show you the way into that state of simple interdependence, of justice, correct alignment with your Source and your brothers.

Many will heed Me, but not all.
Nevertheless, My Army of Light will surely triumph.

Many will see Me soon and know Me not.
Many will see Me soon and recognise Me.
They are My people.
Be you one of them.

My heart flows with Love for you all.

May the Divine Light and Love and Power of the One
God be now manifest within your hearts and minds.
May this manifestation lead you to seek and to know that
Self which is God.

Message No. 5

October 4, 1977

Good evening, My dear friends.

I am pleased indeed to have this further opportunity to speak to you in this way.

My aim is to make known My Presence in the world at the earliest possible moment, and so begin My Work in the full light of day.
This will mean strenuous work by those who now accept that I am among you.
Make known to all that I am here, and pave smooth My path.

My plan is to release into the world a certain Teaching, which will show men that there exists a new approach to living, a new way forward into the future time.

May you be among the first to recognise Me, and through you I may work.

Take upon yourselves this task.
There is none higher which you could do in this life.
Commit yourself to this work and serve your brothers.
I am desirous that the world should know of My Presence, should quickly accept Me, and, hopefully, follow My lead.

I am sure that you will not fail Me.
I am certain that you will not reject this privilege, this gift of service; but will willingly take it upon your shoulders, to ease the burden of My Task.

My Blessings are upon you all.

May the Divine Light and Love and Power of the One
God be now manifest within your hearts and minds.
May this manifestation lead you to know that God dwells
ever within you.
Find That and make It manifest.

Message No. 6

October 11, 1977

Good evening, My dear friends.
Once again, I have the pleasure of speaking to you in this
way.

Very little time indeed now separates Me from you, in
full vision.
Mankind will see Me very soon.

And, if they follow Me, I shall lead them forward into the
future which awaits them:
a future bathed in the light of Truth, of Harmony, and
Love.

My friends, I would ask you to help Me, to take upon
yourselves a share of the burden of preparation.
If you can accept that I am here, make known this fact
wherever you find a listener.

It may be that you will see Me without knowing Me.
It may be that you will walk the other way.

But, if this be so, you will forfeit a treasure unlike that
which you might build in a thousand lifetimes.

Make it your task to tell men that I am here, that I am
working for them, for their future, for the future of all
men and all things in the world.

Make known My Presence among you, and be delivered
of all that is useless in the past.

Make known My Presence, and be assured that My Love
will flow through you and light a path before you for
your brothers and sisters.
Do this work and help them and Me.

My task is but beginning.
When completed, I shall look back on this time as one of
kindling Light in the hearts of the few who sought to
serve their brothers.
May you be one of them.

My heartfelt Love flows to you all.

May the Divine Light and Love and Power of the One
God be now manifest within your hearts and minds.
May this manifestation lead you to seek That which lies
hidden but ever ready to shine forth.
Find That and know God.

Message No. 7

October 20, 1977

Good evening, My dear friends.
I am happy indeed to speak to you once more in this way.

My Plan is working out, but will entail the greatest
service and sacrifice from those among you who accept
that I am in the world.

If you can make known this fact on a wide enough scale,
it will not be long indeed till the world knows My face.

My aim is to shorten this time yet further, but an early
declaration of My Presence depends on you, depends on
your will to serve.

Become My people, and do this work for Me.
Become My friends, and serve your brothers.
Become My children, and know God.

This is no easy task I set you, for men are blind.
But when mankind knows that I am here, I am certain
that it will respond from its heart, and let Me lead.

My people are everywhere.
Join them.
Become one of them.
Make this life a crowning achievement, and take part in
the Great Plan.

I ask you to do this because you have come into the
world for this.

You are here, not by chance, but to serve at this time your brothers and sisters.
Seize then this opportunity, presented to you with love.

My Blessings are upon you all.

May the Divine Light and Love and Power of the One God be now manifest within your hearts and minds. May this manifestation lead you to know that God dwells ever within you. Seek within, and make It manifest.

Message No. 8

October 27, 1977

Once more I have the pleasure of speaking to you
in this way.

My intention is to reveal Myself 'ere long, to send My
Teaching into the world through My people, those who
know Me, who love Me, and through whom I work.

This is the first phase of My Plan.
Then will follow Myself in full vision, known and
recognised or not.
When the world is ready to receive Me, I shall speak to
men everywhere as the One Who is awaited, the One they
have called, the One Who comes to lead them into the
New Age.

My Mission is but beginning, yet, already, there are the
signs of response, of recognition that My Advent is nigh.
Many there are now, throughout the world, who feel My
Presence, who stand open and ready for My Teaching.

When I make Myself known, I shall express the hope of
all mankind for a new life, a new start, a readiness to
change direction; to see the construction of a New World
in which men can live in peace; can live free from fear of
themselves or their brothers; free to create from the joy in
their hearts; free to be themselves, in simple honesty.

My task is but beginning, but even now there exists in
men's hearts a new light, a new hope, a sense of a new
beginning; a realisation that man is not alone, that the
Protector of All has sent His Agent.

It is That which I am.

May the Blessings of Him be upon you all.

May the Divine Light and Love and Power of the One
God, Protector of All, be now manifest within your hearts
and minds.
May this manifestation lead you to know that you are
never without the close Presence and Guidance of God.

Message No. 9

November 3, 1977

Good evening, My dear friends.
I am happy to be with you once more in this fashion, and
to tell you that My Return in full vision will not be long
delayed.

Full well do I know the problems which beset mankind.
Full well do I see the changes required.
But also I see in man the desire to know, to lift his
consciousness, and to see through the clouds.

It is this urge to know which is man's great gift.
When men know the Way to God, this gift will flower in
creative magnificence.

My purpose tonight is to tell you that My Masters are
with you already, are guiding and magnetising the work
of Their groups.
It may be that you yourselves will soon find this stimulus,
recognise it for what it is, and seek to help the Plan.

My Army of Light is assembled, is ready.
Banners flying, eyes uplifted, they march forward into the
future, into the light which beckons, and in that light shall
they see Light.

Many there are who doubt My Presence.
This is natural; men are blind.
But soon there will be no gainsaying.
My efforts will show men that the wheel turns, that soon
the New Time, the New World, will have commenced.
May it be that you will share in this work.

My Blessings are upon you all.

May the Divine Light and Love and Power of the One
and Holy God be now manifest within your hearts and
minds.
May this manifestation lead you to seek and to find That
which dwells ever within you.
Know That as the Self, and make It manifest.

Message No. 10

November 8, 1977

I am among you once more, My dear friends.

I come to tell you that you will see Me very soon, each in his own way.
Those who look for Me in terms of My Beloved Disciple, the Master Jesus, will find His qualities in Me.
Those who look for Me as a Teacher are nearer the mark, for that is what I am.
Those who search for signs will find them, but My method of manifestation is more simple.

Nothing separates you from Me, and soon many will realise this.
I am with you and in you.
I seek to express That which I am through you;
for this I come.

Many will follow Me and see Me as their Guide.
Many will know Me not.
My aim is to enter into the life of all men and, through them, change that life.
Be ready to see Me soon.
Be ready to hear My words,
to follow My thoughts,
to heed My Plea.

I am the Stranger at the Gate.
I am the One Who knocks.
I am the One Who will not go away.

I am your Friend.
I am your Hope.
I am your Shield.
I am your Love.
I am All in All.

Take Me into yourselves, and let Me work through you.
Make Me part of yourselves, and show Me to the world.
Allow Me to manifest through you, and know God.

May the Divine Light and Love and Power of the One
and Holy God be now manifest within your hearts and
minds.
May this manifestation lead you to know that God dwells
silently, now and forever, within you all.

Message No. 11

January 5, 1978

My dear friends, I am happy to be with you once more.

My plan is that My Teaching should precede My
Presence and prepare My way.
My people will release it through their groups and group
endeavour.
When mankind is somewhat prepared, My voice shall be
heard.

Meanwhile, My efforts are bearing fruit, producing
change, drawing together men and nations, and bringing
new hope to the world.

I am emerging soon, but first I would point the way into
the new direction which man, if he would survive, must
take.

Firstly, men must see themselves as brothers, sons of the
One Father.
This is essential if they would progress one step nearer
the Godhead.
Throughout the world there are men, women and little
children who have not even the essentials to stay alive;
they crowd the cities of many of the poorest countries in
the world.
This crime fills Me with shame.
My brothers, how can you watch these people die before
your eyes and call yourselves men?
My plan is to save these, My little ones, from certain
starvation and needless death.

24

My plan is to show you that the way out of your
problems is to listen again to the true voice of God within
your hearts, to share the produce of this most bountiful of
worlds among your brothers and sisters everywhere.

I need your help, I call on you to aid Me in My Task.
How can I stand aside and watch this slaughter, watch My
little ones die?
No, My friends, this cannot be.
Therefore I am come quickly among you once more, to
show you the way, point the Path.
But the success of My Mission depends on you: you must
make the choice — whether you share and learn to live
peacefully as true men, or perish utterly.
My heart tells Me your answer, your choice, and is glad.

May the Divine Light and Love and Power of the One
Most Holy God fall now upon your hearts and minds.
May this Light, Love and Power lead you to seek That
which dwells in silence within you.
Find That and know that you are Gods.

Message No. 12

My dear friends, I am happy to be with you once more,
and to reveal to you My thoughts on man's problem.

Man's problem today, as always, is of his own making; it
is not inherent in the Plan of God.
By the misuse of his divine freewill, man has placed his
future, and that of all the kingdoms, in jeopardy.
Many today are beginning to realise this and are taking
such steps as they can to avert catastrophe.
This is good.
But not all men see the danger which faces mankind in
increasing potency.
Time is short indeed for the reconstruction of our world
along lines more befitting man's true role and purpose.
My task is to show you the way, outline the possibilities
only, for by man himself must the New World be forged.

There are many today who admit the necessity for
change, but still resist it.
There are many today who see the crumbling of the old
and outworn world of the past, but cling to the old forms.

But there is a new voice being heard among the nations:
the voice of Truth, which contains the hope, the promise,
of the New Time.
This voice will increasingly make its impress on the
minds of men, for it is the voice of God, speaking
through men.

My Masters are with you and will show you the way; I
Myself will lead.

Can it be that you will renounce this guidance, this opportunity to rise and progress?

No, My friends, I think not.

I shall show you that the way for man is the way of brotherhood, close co-operation and mutual trust and service.

This is the only way.

All else has failed.

My friends, unless man can do this, man on this Earth will cease to be.

I threaten not, but simply state the truth.

There is but little time left to restore the balance of nature and the world.

Make it your primary task to release to all men the wherewithal to exist in human dignity, as sons of God, brothers all.

Make over, in trust for all men, the produce of the world to the nations of the world.

Do this today as free men, and reap the glory tomorrow as true sons of God.

May the Divine Light and Love and Power of the One Most Holy God fall now upon your hearts and minds. May this Light, Love and Power show you to yourselves as very God.

Message No. 13

January 19, 1978

My dear friends, I am happy indeed to be with you once more in this way.

My Mission is proceeding according to plan and, if all goes well, you will soon hear My voice.
Meanwhile, I would say this:
mankind has lost its way, has strayed far from the path prepared for it by God.
Many there are now in the world who know this, who search and pray, and work towards the light; but many more are blind and would rush towards disaster.
My plan is to halt this headlong plunge and to turn the tide.

My Presence, already, is effecting changes in men's thinking, in men's hearts, and causing them to wonder.
My efforts are proving effective despite all appearances.
Men are turning again to the truth, to the Laws which are God.

Allow Me to show you the way into the New Time; to outline for you the glories, which, if you will, can be yours.
Man is made to serve both God and man, and only through that correct service can the path to God be trodden.
Make it your task to take upon yourselves the task of re-orientation, reconstruction and change.

Each man is a lighthouse and sheds abroad his light for his brother. Make bright your lamp and let it shine forth and show the way.

All are needed, every one.

No one is too small or young to take part in this Great Plan for the rescue and the rehabilitation of our world. Resolve to do this and be assured that My help will not be withheld.

How to start?

Begin by dedicating yourself and all that you are and have been to the service of the world, to the service of your brothers and sisters everywhere.

Make sure that not one day passes without some act of true service and be assured that My help will be yours. This, the Path of Service, is the only path for true men, for it is the path which leads them to God.

My people are drawing together around Me, responding to My Call, and are achieving more than they could know. Together we shall fashion a new and better world.

May you be open and ready for My Call when it comes.

My Blessings are upon you all.

May the Divine Light and Love and Power of the One Most Holy God be now within your hearts and minds. May this Divine Light and Love and Power lead you to become That which you are, true sons of God.

Message No. 14

January 24, 1978

I am with you once more, My dear friends.

My Army of Light is on the march and soon the great
battle will have begun.
My people are preparing My way and will show you My
Plan.
My Masters of Wisdom are now assembling Their various
groups and soon the world will know that I am here.
My Army has laid its plans and soon will follow results.
Already the signs of change are appearing, the clouds are
lifting, and a new hope seizes mankind.

Will you be among those who pave the way?
Will you take part now in this Great Work and fulfil the
world's need?
There is no higher call than that to serve the world.
There is no greater commitment than to serve your
brother.
Hold fast to the purpose of your return and help My Plan.
Many there are who hear Me and heed Me not, but the
few have listened, and with Will and Love fulfil My Task.

There is now assembling a vast army of individuals who
together form My Vanguard.
They know Me, whether they know Me or not.

They follow Me, whether they realise that I am here or
am still to come.
They need Me as I need them.
They are Me, as I am in them.

Make yourselves one of those through whom I may work and reveal Myself.
Take up that challenge and fulfil this life.
Can you not hear the drums calling you into the future?
Can you be deaf to their thunder?
Make now the choice to serve and grow, or forever to regret.

May the Divine Light and Love and Power of the One Most Holy God be now manifest within your hearts and minds.
May this manifestation lead you to seek and to discover the Glory of God which within you dwells.

Message No. 15

My dear friends, I am with you once more.

I am happy to be able to tell you that My Plans proceed smoothly and well.
My Vanguard is preparing mankind and very little time now remains till My face is seen.
I would have you know that I expect all My people, My devoted ones, to work for Me, to prepare somewhat My way.

Many there are now who would gladly know that I am here.
Tell them.
Tell them that the Son of Man has returned, that their Elder Brother is among them, that the long wait is over, and fresh and eager for the battle has come their Friend and Leader.
Tell them this, and offer them too, the opportunity to serve the Plan.

Many will see Me soon and at first may be surprised at My appearance, for I am not the Preacher of Old, but have come simply to point the way, to show the path which must be trodden, back to the Source and into Harmony, Beauty, and Justice.

My task is a simple one: to show you the way.
You, my friends, have the difficult task of building a New World, a New Country, a new Truth; but together we shall triumph.

There are those among you now who know the Way,
have walked the Path before, and can lead and save.
My Brothers, the Masters of Wisdom, are your Friends
and Guides.
They will be among you and serve you and inspire you to
great deeds, valiant acts; and They bring precious gifts of
Wisdom and Love to place at your feet.

There is only one way to God and that, My friends, you
already know.
The way to God is the way of Brotherhood, of Justice and
Love.
There is no other way; all is contained therein.
Many will find this Path bitter and hard; but many more,
by far, will enter upon this Path with joy and gladness at
the lightness of their burden, casting away the old, the
outworn and the useless, the trivia of the past; and
entering into shared brotherhood and joyous communion
with all that is, that vast and growing Company shall
inherit their Selfhood.

May the Divine Light and Love and Power of the One
and Holy God be now manifest within your hearts and
minds.
May this manifestation lead you to seek and to know that
within you dwells, now and forever, that God which is
your Self.

Message No. 16

February 7, 1978

My dear friends, I am happy to be with you once more.

My plan is to reveal to men that there exists for them but two paths.
One will lead them inexorably to devastation and death.
The other, My friends, My dear ones, will lead mankind straight to God; and in the light of His Presence they, if ready, will see wonders and unbelievable glories.

My task is to point the way, to lead you out of discord into that blessed state of Harmony and Love which will vouchsafe to you that dream.
My Work proceeds, and soon, now very soon, you will see My face and hear My words.

The period of test begins.
My plan is to place before you these two alternatives, to outline the possibilities and the pitfalls.
The choice is yours; you, from your own divinely given free will, must decide.
If you, as in My heart I know you will, decide for God, I shall take you to Him; and together we shall place before Him our life of service to Him and to the world.
Many of My people, already, are so doing.
It is this which confers on them the appellation, "My beloved ones".
Join this band of true servers of the world.

Become My workers;
become My companions;
become My heroes, and serve the Plan.

Little time remains for this work of preparation.
Take now the first steps into your glory.
Serve the purpose of your return and the Plan of God:
they are one and the same.
My Masters will show you the first steps out of the
quagmire. They will show you that a simpler life can be
led in full happiness and manifested divinity, through
Love and Service of our brothers.
This is the Way of Old; it is the way of all
time; nothing really changes with God.
Make now your choice: to serve My Plan and see the
Light which beckons you into the future, or to sound
forever the knell of regret.

May the Divine Light and Love and Power of the One
Most Holy God be now manifest within your hearts and
minds.
May this manifestation lead you to look within and there
to find that God Who forever in you dwells.

Message No. 17

February 14, 1978

Good evening, My dear friends, I am happy to be with you once more in this way.

Soon My Appearance will be known to many and My Teaching will have begun.
Mankind will be faced by Me with two lines of action; on their decision rests the future of this world.
I will show them that the only possible choice is through sharing and mutual interdependence.
By this means, man will come into that state of awareness of himself and his purpose which will lead him to the feet of God.
The other way is too terrible to contemplate, for it would mean the annihilation of all lifestreams on this Earth.

Man has the future in his hands.
Weigh well, oh men, and if you choose as true men would, I may lead you into the Light of your divine inheritance.
Make your choice well, and let Me lead.
Make your choice well, and be assured of My continuing succour.
Make your choice well, My brothers, and be delivered of all that holds you in limitation.

My Army is on the move, is marching bravely into the future.
Join those who already fight on the side of Light, on the side of Truth, of Freedom and Justice.
Join My Vanguard and show the way for your brothers.

Many there are who sense that I am here, yet speak not. Why hold this knowledge to yourself when your brothers cry for light, for wisdom, and help?

Allow them, too, to share in the joy of the Promise which I bring.

Tell them, My friends, that you believe that Maitreya has come; that the Lord of Love is here; that the Son of Man walks again among His brothers.

Tell them that soon My face will be seen, My words will be heard; and in the seeing and the hearing, they are tested and known.

May the Divine Light and Love and Power of the One Most Holy God be now manifest within your hearts and minds.

May this manifestation lead you to seek and to find that Divine Source from which you came.

Message No. 18

My dear friends, I am indeed happy to be with you once more.

My face will soon be seen, My words heard.
When you see Me, you will know that you have not waited in vain.
You will know that your Brother of Old has come to share your life.

Liberation is the goal for mankind.
To that goal I shall point the way, shall lead you forward, and cut before you the steps of ascent.

My Masters will show you how to live simply and well and in full happiness.
They have trodden the road before and know well the way.

Like children in full trust, let Them show you that Way; let Them take you step by step through the labyrinth.
And when you are ready, before My Splendour shall you come, and through Me shall you see the face of God.

Make your choice well, My friends; make it now.
Take your stand with those who wish to share and love, with those for whom Justice is divine.
Make now your choice and let your light shine forth and ease My path.

Men await My Coming yet know not that I am already here.
Tell them that My Manifestation is completed.

I, Maitreya, their Brother, stand among them.
Await My Call, and act.
Tell men that I expect that they will follow Me, but they must decide.
They must want the Path which they must tread if they would see God.

May the Divine Light and Love and Power of the One Most Holy God be now manifest within your hearts and minds.
May this manifestation lead you to seek and to find that Joy and Peace which forever in you dwells.

Message No. 19

February 28, 1978

Good evening, My dear friends.
I am happy indeed to be with you once more and to tell
you that I emerge forthwith.

The time of My Coming is over.
The time of My Emergence has arrived; and soon, now,
in full vision and fact, My face and words will become
known.
May you quickly recognise Me, My dear friends, My dear
ones, and help your brothers to do likewise.

I am your Friend and Brother, not a God.
It is true that My Father has, once again, sent Me to you;
but I come to you who are My brethren, to guide you and
lead you, if you will, into a blessed future.
My task will be to show you that for mankind the ways
part.
The signposts are set, and on your decision rests the
future of this Earth.
We are here together, you and I, to ensure that man
chooses the correct path, the only Way which can lead
him to God.

You are here because in your heart you are responding to
My Call, to the fact of My Presence, knowingly or not.
Make it then your task to tell the others, to point to the
simple way of Truth which beckons mankind.
Teach men that to share is divine; to love is God's nature;
to work together is man's destiny.

Take your stand on the only platform from which the
Light of the future may be seen.
Take your stand, My friends, together, and show the way.

Many of you will see Me soon.
Share with your brothers this joyous expectation and tell
them that Maitreya, their Friend, their Brother, their
Teacher of Old, has come.
Do this now and restore to men the hope which they have
lost.
Do this now and work for Me.
Work in service to the world and stand in the blessing of
My Love.

May the Divine Light and Love and Power of the One
Most Holy God be now manifest within your hearts and
minds.
May this manifestation reveal to you that you are, now
and forever, sons of the only living God.

Message No. 20

March 7, 1978

My dear friends, I am with you once more.

I wish to tell you that My Presence in the world will soon be known to many, My face seen and My Teaching heard.

I am with you in many ways:
I am with you as Maitreya, the Leader of My group of Masters.
I am with you as the Embodiment of that Divine Force which you call the Christ Principle.
I am with you as your Brother of Old, as the Eldest of our family.
I am with you as God's Representative, as the Spokesman for that Divine Being Whose dreams we are.
I shall take you to Him when you are ready, when you have passed through the Gates twice, and stood shining before Me.

My friends, I am with you and in you and around you.
I am the Lord of Love.
I am the Hope of Mankind.
I am the Well.
I am your Bliss.
I am returned to you by the One we call God.

May the Divine Light and Love and Power of the One Most Holy God be now manifest within your hearts and minds.

May this manifestation lead you to seek and to know that Divine Self which, now and forever, you are.

Message No. 21

March 14, 1978

My dear friends, I am happy indeed to be with you once more in this fashion.

My plan is that My face and words shall be known forthwith.
My Emergence begins.
May it be that you will quickly sense My Presence, seek Me out and share My burden, for My Plan involves you all.
There is little that I can do without your help, your eager participation and acceptance of service.
Through you, if you know Me, love Me, love My Work, answer My Call, that work may be done.
I need helpers.
I seek to place before you the chance to grow in Service, to lift yourselves upward into a new Light, into a new responsibility, and when I call, I shall expect you.
Many there are now who are doing this work for Me yet know Me not, nor know that I am here.
It has always been so, for many work better in the shade.
But you, My friends, have the opportunity for full and conscious service.
Seize it then and begin now.
Take part in a Great Plan which is changing the world, which is drawing together all men and all nations, which is showing the way into the future and back to God.

Many of you have heard this Call before, yet still resist action.

Nothing will happen by chance.
It is a Call to Action that I give and that action will I potentise, manyfold.
Take now this chance to be My disciples, to be My friends, My true men.

Before My Coming, men knew no way out; stuck fast in the quagmire of their problems, they feared.
Today there is a new light, a new possibility for change.
A new hope is sweeping the world: that is My Ray, my Gift to you, My Blessing to all men.

May the Divine Light and Love and Power of the One Most Holy God be now manifest within you all.

Message No. 22

March 22, 1978

I am with you once more, My dear friends.

I am here to tell you that My Emergence has commenced, and before long you will see Me and hear My words.

There are those among you who know that I am here, who see Me in their visions and dreams, yet speak not. Why hold this wonder to yourselves? My people cry for truth, for light and succour. Let them know that I am returned, that I am here, working and planning for them; to take them, if they will, back to the Father, onward into the future, upward into the Light. Tell them that I am among them and soon will they see Me. Tell them this.

My Plans work smoothly, and soon you will see a great transformation in the world. Despite the signs, the changes are occurring. Despite the tension, My Love is spread abroad. Know this and be at peace within yourselves and raise the hope of men.

I am here with you now, My dear friends, and ask you to give Me your allegiance, your trust, your help.

To show men that the way into the future lies through Love and Justice, have I come. To take men into that future and to show them the Ways of God, am I here.

Be then, My dear ones, ready to receive Me, to work with Me, to dispel the fog of fear and ignorance which enshrouds mankind.
Take, then, My hand, and let Me lead you into that golden future in which those who are ready shall see the face of God.
My Blessing goes with you all.

May the Divine Light and Love and Power of the One Most Holy God be now manifest within your hearts and minds.
May this manifestation lead you to seek and to find that Divine Being Whom in truth you are.

Message No. 23

March 28, 1978

Good evening, My dear friends.
I am happy to be with you once more and to reveal to
you My Plan for the immediate future time.

My plan is to make known My face in full and visible
fact, to reach you through My words, to receive from you
your allegiance and help.
Naught can be done by Me without this willing help, for
you, My friends, must remake the world.
I shall send My Disciples to you, and They will show you
the way; but you must act and follow Our Plan.

My Teaching will proceed from now.
Gradually men will know of My Presence, take heed, and
begin to follow a new course.
My hope is that you will quickly gather yourselves
around Me, wherever you may be, and take your stand by
My side.
Men and women throughout the world, who share My
hope for a new life for men, will lead the way; and
together we shall make safe the world.

My Vanguard has been preparing mankind for this time.
There are few in the world who know not in their hearts
that My Return is nigh.
On all levels this truth resounds.

You will find this to be so when you make your approach
to your brothers. Each one of you in his heart has seen the
new light which beckons from afar, which holds the
Promise of the future time.

That light will grow into a flame unseen before on Earth, when mankind takes the Path which will lead him back to God.
That Path it is My Mission to unfold before your advancing feet and point the way to God.

May the Divine Light and Love and Power of the One Most Holy God be now manifest within your hearts and minds.
May this manifestation lead you out of the labyrinth into the light; that you might grow in that light, and see a higher Light.

Message No. 24

April 4, 1978

My dear friends, I am happy to be with you once more in this way.

Soon will you see Me in full fact.
My Presence will become known to you, and, if your response is as I hope, we shall meet and work together as friends.
My intention is to place before you the answers to man's dilemma, to show you that the future holds for all men unbelievable promise.
With My Brothers, the Masters of Wisdom, I shall show you the way to release your divinity and receive your inheritance.

My plan is to awaken mankind to its true worth, its true capacity, and show it that within all men lives a divine son of God.
If men will follow Me, I shall take them step by step through the process of Initiation, whose Seal I guard.
In this way, they will reveal the God Who within them dwells.

My Masters are preparing the way.
They are choosing Their workers through whom to act, and soon, in the centres, the Fiat will go forth, the work will commence, and the New Dispensation for mankind will begin.

You who are here present are among those who can point the way. Show to your brothers that there exists for man a better life, a better future than he could dream of.

Tell them that Maitreya lives, that the Lord of Love walks abroad, that the Son of Man is returned to the world, to change that world, through men.
Tell them this, My friends, and reveal to them the hope of the future.

May the Divine Light and Love and Power of the One Most Holy God be now manifest within your hearts and minds.
May this manifestation lead you to seek and to find that God Who forever you have been.

Message No. 25

April 11, 1978

My dear friends, I am with you once more.

I can tell you now that there are those among your
brothers and sisters who have seen My face. My name as
yet is unknown to them but My Presence is a living
reality to them.
May this soon be so for you.

My Masters are gathering together Their forces, Their
groups, and in focussed strength We move forward into
the future, into the light of a new day.
My aim is to take you with Me into that clear Light, and
to spread before your eyes the wonders of God.
Take heart from these words, My friends, and follow Me.
Let Me lift you upwards into your true stature as sons of
God, as true men, brothers all.
I hold out My hands towards you, ready to receive you
with love, to show you the way which all men must
sometime tread.
Take then, My hands, My dear ones, and let Me lead.

Make known to all that I am here, that I am returned and
prepare men for the Day of Declaration, the day of God's
Gift; for on that day, men will celebrate together the
achievement of God's Will.
My Coming is nothing less.

Take now your stand at My side, and let us together
prove that man is God, that there is nothing which is
other than God.

May the Divine Light and Love and Power of the One
Most Holy God be now manifest within your hearts and
minds.
May this manifestation lead you to realise your true
nature as sons of God.

Message No. 26

April 18, 1978

My dear friends, I am happy to be with you once more.

I am indeed among you, in a new way: your brothers and
sisters know Me, have seen Me and call Me Friend and
Brother.

My plan is to reveal Myself stage by stage, and to draw
together around Me those enlightened souls through
whom I may work.
This process has begun, and soon, in My centre, My
Presence will become known.

My body of workers will show the world that the
problems of mankind can be solved.
Through the process of sharing and just redistribution, the
needs of all can be met.
This growing group will show men that there is but little
need for the suffering of so many, for the hunger, disease
and anguish which beset mankind.

My plan is to take you on a journey into a New Country,
a new approach to living in which all men can share.
Let Me lead you, let Me show you the way,
let Me lift you upwards into the light of a
New Truth.
Let Me show you, My friends, the Way to God, for only
through the manifestation of God's Will can God be
known.
I am here to administer that Will.

Take this opportunity to serve and grow in Service, My friends, for none greater has been offered to any man. Take this opportunity to serve, and see the face of Him we call God.

My arms are held towards you, My friends, asking for your trust, appealing for your help in remaking your world.
Many are the tasks which lie ahead, many are the blows which must be struck for Freedom and Truth.
I need all those in whom that truth shines to follow Me and help Me in My Work.
May you be ready when you hear My Call.
That Call will resound in the ears of men everywhere, throughout the world.
It is a Call to God.

May the Divine Light and Love and Power of the One Most Holy God be now manifest within your hearts and minds.
May this manifestation lead you to seek and to know that Essence of God which in truth you are.

Message No. 27

April 25, 1978

I am happy to be with you again, My dear friends, and to
tell you that My Emergence proceeds to plan.

There are many now among your brothers who know Me
well, who trust Me, whose Advocate I shall become.

Make haste to welcome Me, to know Me, to share My
burden.
Those among you who wish to serve the world have
placed before them now the opportunity of all lives. May
you seize it, use it to the full, and create for yourselves
and your brothers a new life.

My people are preparing My way.
Make yourselves one with them, help them, keep close
contact with their work and let them show you the way.

My Plan runs smoothly.
My Purposes are being fulfilled.
My Rule is being approached.
My Time is near.
My Law will be established.
My Love is spread abroad.
My Teaching will show men the way forward,
the only way left to them,
the Way of Old,
the Way of God,
the Way of True Men, True Sons of God.

My Love will be established in the hearts of men and
together in Love we shall know God, see the face of Him
Who sits on the Shining Throne.
Together we shall kneel at His feet and know the Peace of
God.
That is My Task.
Let Me take you there, My friends and brothers.
Respond quickly to My Presence and Teaching, and I
may lead you before the Throne.

Make haste, My friends, all is well. All is fast being
accomplished.
My Mission shall flourish.

May the Divine Light and Love and Power of the One
Most Holy God be now manifest within your hearts and
minds.
May this manifestation lead you to see that you are but
aspects of God.

Message No. 28

May 9, 1978

I am with you once more, My dear friends.

I would like to show you a new way to live, a way based
on the innate brotherhood of man, on his capacity to love
and share, and on his essential divinity.

The process of becoming divine is a simple one, a natural
one, open freely to all men.
It is the process of releasing that God Who, from the
beginning, has dwelt within you.
My Promise is this: if you will follow Me into the New
Time, I shall release for you your divine nature.
I am the Way and the Means to God, for I guard the
Gates through which all men pass to come to the feet of
God.
If you can trust Me to show you the Way, I shall lead you
forward and upward and take you to Him.
That is My Task.

I tell you only what you already know: that men are
brothers; but when that brotherhood becomes manifest in
the world, that divinity likewise shall shine forth.

My Emergence proceeds.
Many now there are who know Me and call Me Friend,
who salute Me daily, whose smile of welcome I cherish.
Soon I shall be known to you in a certain fashion,
outlining for you the possibilities of change.
May you quickly see Me, know Me and work for Me.

My plan is to show Myself to the world so soon now that there will remain but little doubt that the Lord of Love is here, that the Son of Man is among you, that the Prince of Peace has returned.

May the Divine Light and Love and Power of the One Most Holy God be now manifest within your hearts and minds.
May this manifestation lead you to seek and know that Divine Light within your heart which is very God.

Message No. 29

May 16, 1978

My dear friends I am happy to be with you once more
and to release to you a fragment of My Teaching.

My Masters will teach you the rules of Life; I Myself will
show you that higher Light which beckons mankind.
My Teaching is twofold: it has to do with man's physical
nature, the necessities of life; it has to do, also, with
man's relationship to that Divine Being Whom we call
God.
In My vocabulary these are as one, for only in so far as
man correctly relates to man does he so relate to God.
My plan is to show you this, to teach you that when man
discovers in himself the ability to share, to love, to trust,
from that moment begins his ascent to God.
It was always so and always shall be so.

My Coming has been expected by millions.
My Arrival among you is known to relatively few.
Nevertheless, these few can tell the others and light in
them the joy which My Promise brings.

My Mission is now under way, achieving results.
Soon, in My centre, My face and name will be known
and will attract to Me those who seek to serve.
May you be among them.

My precise abode is not so important.
What you should look for is My Message, My Call, and
respond from your heart.

My Task begins well and soon you shall see the creation of a new map, of a New Country.
That Country I call Love.

May the Divine Light and Love and Power of the One Most Holy God be now manifest within your hearts and minds.
May this manifestation lead you to seek and to find that Divine Spark which in truth you are.

Message No. 30

May 23, 1978

My dear friends, I am happy to be with you once more.

My Plan runs smoothly; My work proceeds and now, in
My centre, My name and face are known to many.
Your brothers seek My help and bring to Me their
troubles.
I welcome this and soon shall stand for them in greater
stead.

My Masters are working now to bring about the
transformation of your social life, the old forms of which
are rotten and perished.
Under Their guidance, your brothers are preparing the
new forms, the new lines of action, through which may be
expressed the new aspirations of man in this New Age.

Allow Me to tell you this: My Mission is proceeding so
well now that soon the world will know — that the
Forerunner has returned, that the Way of Truth is open,
that the Light of the future beckons,
that the cry of man has been heard,
that the Plan of God works out,
that the signs of the New can be seen,
that the Love of God shall be expressed.
My Coming is the guarantee of all of this.

I am the Answer to the past.
I am the Hope for the future.
I am the Lamp.

I am the Path to God.
I am the Secret One.
I am the Foundation.
I am the Presence.

Join your brothers in service to Me and to the world.
Prepare for My Emergence and create a new and happier
world for all men.
Do this now, My friends.
Prepare to see Me soon.
Prepare to acknowledge Me.
Prepare to sound the note of triumph of the Truth.

May the Divine Light and Love and Power of the
Everlasting God be now manifest within your hearts and
minds.
May this manifestation lead you to be ever within the
Aura of the Living God.

Message No. 31

May 30, 1978

My dear friends, I am happy to be with you once more.

My Plan proceeds well. I am among friends, your brothers know Me and love Me, and for them shall I speak.

When you see Me you will know why I have come, for I shall appeal to you in these terms:
"Save My little ones.
Feed your brothers.
Remember that mankind is One, children of the One Father.
Make over, in trust, the goods of the Earth to all who are in need.
Do this now and save the world."

Thus shall I speak; so shall be My Appeal; and when mankind has accepted this Law, I shall declare Myself.
Many there are now who know this to be true, who desire to share, who long for brotherhood, yet act not.
Nothing happens by itself. Man must act and implement his will.
Today, that will is the Will, also, of God.
Therefore, the outcome is assured.

My brothers, why wait for My Appearance?
Why sit still when the world groans; when men, women and children die in misery, cast off by their brothers?
There is no greater aspiration than the desire to serve.
Make your act of service the saving of the starving of the world and help My Plan.

My Army is arrayed, in position; the Light of Truth
shines in their eyes, and at the Call from Me, it will act.
See yourselves as one of that Company of Light and be
assured that My Love will act through you.
Make yourselves one of that joyous Company and be
assured of My strength.
Take up the challenge which this service presents and be
fulfilled in this life.

My Mission is beginning but already the wheels are
turning, the blueprint of Truth descends and My Light
shines in the hearts of men.

May the Divine Light and Love and Power of the One
and Holy God be now manifest within your hearts and
minds.
May this manifestation lead you to be that Centre of Light
which in truth you are.

Message No. 32

June 13, 1978

My dear friends, I am with you once more.

My Appearance among men is nigh.
Soon, for yourselves, you will know that I am with you.
Your brothers, already, know Me and trust Me and look
to Me as Leader.
In this fashion shall I speak for them and to the world,
placing before mankind the choices.

Many hear Me even now, listen to My words and ponder,
for I tell them what in their hearts they know.
I tell them that Justice is a Law of God.
I tell them that Love is the Way to the Source.
I show them that without Love and Justice, mankind will
perish.

My brothers love Me for these Truths, for they recognise
them to stand behind all life.
Thus shall I speak and thus shall you know that I am
among you. Make haste to follow Me, to create the New
Time, the glorious future which shines ahead for mankind.

Let Me speak to you simply, My friends.
Let Me trace for you the Plan of God for that future.
Let Me show you the way to manifest that God which
you are, and so complete that Plan.

Perhaps you are surprised by the fact of My early Return,
but men and women weep, children die, and others laugh
in blind forgetfulness.

My Coming is not by chance but by Law and Love.
That Law and that Love have brought Me here.
When you see Me you will see a Friend and Brother, and
I shall know My Coming has not been in vain.

May the Divine Light and Love and Power of the One
Most Holy God be now manifest within your hearts and
minds.
May this manifestation lead you to see your true nature as
Love.

Message No. 33

June 22, 1978

My dear friends, I am happy to be with you once more.

Many will see Me soon, will hearken to My words, and follow My lead.
May you be among the first to do so, for in this way you can become My co-workers.
My need for such is great.
Many there are who share My hope for the restoration of our world.
Seek them out and work with them.
Build together a stronghold of Light and illumine the path for your brothers.
Sit not still, but act, and restore the Time of Truth.
My Masters will point the Path for you and under Their guidance you can create great achievements.

My purpose tonight is to tell you that My methods are simple indeed.
My plan is this: to place before mankind the alternatives of sharing and death.
No-one in truth could for mankind choose the latter, for that death would be shameful and bitter indeed, unlike your blackest fears.
My friends, there is a way of Hope.
There is a way into the Light.
That simple way lies through Brotherhood and Love.
Many times before have you heard this.
Nevertheless, mankind yet awaits its fulfilment.

Make then, gladly, your choice for Life, for Justice and Sharing, and follow Me into your most glorious and shining future.

Make this your choice, My friends, and be endowed with your true stature as very Gods.

May the Divine Light and Love and Power of the One Most Holy God be now manifest within your hearts and minds.

May this manifestation lead you to seek and to find that Centre of Silence within you all.

Message No. 34

June 29, 1978

My dear friends, I am with you once more and am happy to speak to you in this way.

I am with you in a very real sense, but soon you will see Me more clearly and, when you do, you will see your Friend and Elder Brother.
My Mission proceeds rhythmically and well and My Plans are, without doubt, receiving due response from mankind.
Many there are now who heed Me without the knowledge of My Presence, but the hearts of men respond and soon a great transformation will take place in the world.
Many are sensing My Presence, however obliquely, and heeding My Call.
Through them I work, through them My Plan works out.

When I make My Declaration before mankind, many will realise that in their hearts they saw Me.
When that day comes I shall look upon you all, brothers and sisters, as workers for the Light and engage you in the transforming of our world.

When I announce Myself to the world, I shall speak to all men in these terms:
"Prepare to see yourselves as Gods.
Prepare to be uplifted into Light.
Prepare to realise yourselves as brothers, one of another.
Prepare to teach the Truth.
Prepare to live the Law.
Welcome this Law and restore the Plan of God."

May the Divine Light and Love and Power of the One
Most Holy God be now manifest within your hearts and
minds.
May this manifestation lead you to seek and to find that
Essence of Truth which forever you have been.

Message No. 35

July 6, 1978

My dear friends, I am happy to be with you once more.

My Plans work out.
My Emergence takes a little time but proceeds well.
Soon, among your brothers, My Teaching will begin and,
resounding through the world, will usher in a New Age.

My Promise holds: I shall take before the Throne of God
all who can follow Me into the Higher Light which I
bring.
May you be among those who shall know this joy.
Take your place by My side and together shall we make
all things new.
Take My hand, My friends, and let Me guide you through
My Garden,
Let Me show you My Flowers.
Let Me teach you My Law.

My heart enfolds you as always and on each step of the
upward path, My hand steadies and guides.
I am your Master, Brother and Friend.
Know Me then in this way.

Let Me teach you the simple Path to God.
Let Me show you the Greater Light Divine.
Let us travel together this Path and know the Secrets of
Old, know the Wonders of God, know the Blessing of
Love.

The cry for Justice from men has reached My ears and to that cry I hearken.

The call for succour has risen to Me and I hasten to give.

The pain of the world sits heavily on My heart and this gladly would I lighten.

My pain can be yours; My burden can be shared. I offer you both.

Take My pain, My brothers, and turn it into Joy.

Ease My burden, My friends, and know Bliss.

May the Divine Light and Love and Power of the One Most Holy God be now manifest within your hearts and minds.

May this manifestation lead you to see that you are always and ever centres in the Being of God.

Message No. 36

July 13, 1978

I am with you once more, My dear friends.

All is well.
My planned Emergence is taking place and within a short
time, in My centre, My face will be known.
The first phase has been successfully completed and in
joy may you await My Teaching.
When you see Me, you will know that the time has come
for change.
The world awaits the sounding of the Cosmic Dates.
The nations prepare for a New Dispensation and in Trust
and Brotherhood all men will share.

My Masters are now emerging more quickly than
planned; this stimulus will bring great benefits to the
world, conveying as They do the Love of God.
My Masters will help you to manifest this Divine Love,
will show you the simple Way of Truth, the blessing of
Trust.

Be not afraid, My friends, for all will be well.
The New Light shines, the New Country beckons, and in
that Country I shall show you the wonders of God.
Be ready to follow Me therein and be enabled to manifest
your God-given greatness.

May the Divine Light and Love and Power of the One Most Holy God be now manifest within your hearts and minds.

May this manifestation lead you to be ever enfolded in the indwelling Light and Love of God.

Message No. 37

July 18, 1978

My dear friends, I am pleased indeed to speak to you once more.

My Mission goes well.
My heart fills with joy at the prospect of My renewed contact with My brothers.
All who love and serve their brothers I think of in this way.

My immediate plan is to reveal Myself stage by stage in a certain fashion, and, broadening My field of work, speak for all men.
Soon I shall be among you in a way unmistakable to your prepared hearts.
By this means will you know Me: by My Light which shines through you, awakening you to service and Love.
By this means will you know Me: by My Call for Justice and Reason.
By this means shall you know Me: by My work among your brothers, those who need My help.
My Appeal shall sound forth: "Save the world, help those who suffer and die in need."
My Call shall resound: "Correct the mistakes of the past and renew the spirit of man.
Make way for Love in your hearts and see God."
Thus shall I speak, My friends, and thus will you know Me.

My Task begins, a task which for long have I planned in wisdom and joy, a task which for Me is the fulfilment of My Mission and the fulfilment of the Will of God.

May the Divine Light and Love and Power of the One Most Holy God be now manifest within your hearts and minds.

May this manifestation lead you to be ever mindful of your true splendour as Sparks of God.

Message No. 38

July 25, 1978

I am with you once more, My dear friends.

I am happy to be able to tell you that there are those
among your brothers who have seen Me and have given
Me their allegiance. They trust Me to show them the
forward path, that Path which leads upward into the Light
of God.
Let Me take you with Me into that Divine Light, to show
you the marvels which await your astonished eyes.
My dear children, I would like to show you that to love
God and to love man are the same; as we love our
brothers, so do we manifest our love of God.
Theoretically you know this, but, My dear friends, the
practice of love is essential, for by Love alone will this
Earth be sustained.

My efforts are proving successful in changing the balance
in the world.
Men are ready to receive Me; knowingly or not, they
await My Presence.
Daily I hearken to their prayers.

My Masters are among you in a new way, closer to you
than ever before, sowing the seeds of Love and Trust
among the nations.
May it be that these seeds of Love shall find fertile soil.
My plan is to emerge forthwith, to speak to the people
simply and in language which all men may understand; to
speak to them as brothers, to guide their footsteps in the
direction of God.

God may be known by many names:
I call Him Love;
I call Him also Justice.
Both Love and Justice are the foundation of our life.
Seek Me out and know your Brother of Old.
Hearken to My Message, My friends, and together in joy
shall we transform this world.

May the Divine Light and Love and Power of the One
Most Holy God be now manifest within your hearts and
minds.
May this manifestation lead you to be ever enfolded in
the ever-flowing Blessing and Love of God.

Message No. 39

August 1, 1978

My dear friends, I am with you once more, and happy I am to be so.

My Teaching goes forth. My words resound on all planes, and act to bring Light to mankind.
Soon, in My centre, men will awake to find among them the Son of Man, for, My friends, My Mission proceeds and My steps are sounding the New Time.
Your brothers know Me, accept Me for One of themselves and make Me at home in the world.
When you see Me, you will find a Brother and Friend, a Teacher and Guide, a Refuge and Shield.
Look for My Emergence soon and be prepared to work for Me, to show your brothers the way forward, the way into the Light, the way to know the Secrets of God.

To show you these have I come.
To teach you the simple Truths am I here.
To lead you into the Blessed Country of Love have I returned.
Make it your task to find Me quickly, to light the lamp of your brother, to send My words into the world to reach your brother's heart.
May you be among those who quickly find and recognise Me, for, if you do, you may become My warriors.

My Task begins.
It is a task for which I have waited long, but one which I shoulder with joy.
My Army is now on the move and soon the clash of battle will be heard.

The outcome of this battle is assured, for at My side are true sons of God.

Take your places in the ranks of My Army, My friends, and create the New Time, the Time of God.

May the Divine Light and Love and Power of the One Most Holy God be now manifest within your hearts and minds.

May this manifestation lead you to be ever mindful that you are, now and forever, children of God.

Message No. 40

August 8, 1978

My dear friends, I am happy to be with you once more.

I shall soon be known to you in more complete fashion and you will know for yourselves that I am among you.

My Love is changing the world.
Today, men stand ready for a new life, a new principle, the principle of Love.
That is My Gift to you.

My Army is ready for battle, My Masters of Wisdom and Myself at the head.
That battle will be fought for the continuance of man on this Earth.
Rest assured that My Army shall triumph.

My Law will be accepted by men.
My Love will blossom in their hearts, and through this Law of Love, mankind will know God.
My Teaching will show you the way to God, the simple path of Justice and Love.
My Masters will teach you the ancient Laws and Lore, and bring you before Me.

I am the Light.
I am the Law.
I am the Ascended One.
I am the Knower of God's Will.
I am the Beacon.
I am the Support of all men.

I know men's hearts and seek to purify them.
I know men's cares and seek to help them.
I know the anguish of many and return to save them.

My brothers and friends, I am with you and around you.
I am your loving heart.
I am your highest thought.
I am your pity.

Manifest That which I am and know the bliss which
comes to those who know God.

May the Divine Light and Love and Power of the One
Most Holy God be now manifest within your hearts and
minds.
May this manifestation lead you into the arms of the
Everlasting God.

Message No. 41

September 7, 1978

My dear friends, I am happy to be with you once more.

You shall see Me soon, and when you do, without doubt you will know that your Brother, Maitreya Himself, is among you.

I am with you in many ways, chief among these as the Embodiment of Love.
This principle of Love underlies all Being, and without its manifestation, Life would cease to be.
My Mission is to evoke the principle of Love in all men, and for those who are ready, to show a Higher Truth.

The means are simple:
through Justice and Freedom for all, that Love can be expressed.
Through the manifestation of man's Brotherhood, the Source of All can be known.
May it be that you will quickly see this, understand the purpose of life and show the way for your brothers.
Thus can you take part in the transformation of your world.

My Masters are developing, through Their groups, new forms and structures for your life.
These will allow you better to express the Divine Beings which you are, and thus complete the Plan.
Take part, My friends, in this great adventure of Spirit, and allow Me to show you, and lead you into, your heritage.

May the Divine Light and Love and Power of the One
Most Holy God be now manifest within your hearts and
minds.
May this manifestation bring you swiftly and surely to the
feet of God.

Message No. 42

My dear friends, I am happy to be with you once more.

Many times have you heard Me say that My Coming
means change.
Specifically, the greatest change will be in the hearts and
minds of men, for My Return among you is a sign that
men are ready to receive new life.
That New Life for men do I bring in abundance.
On all the planes this Life will flow, reaching the hearts
and souls and bodies of men, bringing them nearer to the
Source of Life Itself.
My task will be to channel those Waters of Life through
you.

I am the Water Carrier.
I am the Vessel of Truth.
That Truth shall I reveal to you and lift you into your true
nature.

I am the River.
Through Me flows the new stream of God-given Life, and
this shall I bestow on you.
Thus shall we together walk through My Garden, smell
the perfume of My Flowers, and know the joy of
closeness to God.

My friends, these things are not dreams.
All of this will be yours.
My Mission will vouchsafe this to you.

May the Divine Light and Love and Power of the One
Most Holy God be now manifest within your
hearts and minds.
May this manifestation take you into the lap of the
Everlasting God.

Message No. 43

September 19, 1978

My dear friends, I am happy to be with you once more.

My Pledge will be fulfilled.
I shall take before the Shining One all who can follow Me
into the Higher Light, and in this way shall you see the
face of God.

My friends, God is nearer to you than you can imagine.
God is yourself.
God is within you and all around you.
God also sits in majesty on the Golden Throne, and when
you are ready, we shall kneel together at His divine feet.
Thus shall it be.
Make haste to follow Me therefore, to reach the heights
from which can be seen the glories of God, the Blessed
Country of Love, the River of Truth.
Allow Me to take you with Me into that fair land and
show you the wonders of your inheritance.

My Masters are training Their groups to show the way to
implement man's needs.
Through this manifestation, all goodness will follow.
My Masters know the problems which beset man today;
the answers likewise are in Their grasp.
Allow Them to lead, My friends, and show you the
simple path of Joy, Simplicity and Truth.

A new Law descends.
The new Truth becomes known to man.
The Law is Love,
The Truth, My friends, is Brotherhood.

My Mission will ensure that that Law and that Truth shall become manifest.
This I promise you and thus shall it be.

May the Divine Light and Love and Power of the One Most Holy God be now manifest within your hearts and minds.
May this manifestation lead you to be ever enfolded by the Living God.

Message No. 44

September 26, 1978

My dear friends, I am happy to be with you once again,
and to tell you that My Emergence proceeds well.

My face is known to a growing number of your brothers,
but My name for the present must remain undisclosed.
In this way, My secret can be maintained.
Why should this be so?
To enable you, My friends and brothers, to find Me from
the light within you, that Light which I bring.
You must know and want That for which I stand.
Within your hearts must burn the desire for Justice and
Truth.
Where these divine aspects are present, you will recognise
Me.
I envisage little difficulty for those who follow My Law,
for this Law evokes within you the desire for Truth.

My Presence is causing such changes in the world that
before long the knowledge of My Existence will be
ascertained.
Men will raise the question: how can it be; from where
does this new light shine?
The divisions of old will merge and grow together; the
sons of men will sense a higher light and, turning their
faces towards that Light, shall find Me waiting to lead
them.
Thus shall it be.
Thus shall the truth in the hearts of men respond to the
Truth which I am.
Thus shall that new Light be kindled in their hearts, and
the anguish of men depart.

This time, My friends, is near.
This time, My brothers, is almost upon you.
Wake to the fact of My Presence!
Wake to the promise of your deliverance!

May the Divine Light and Love and Power of the One
Most Holy God be now manifest within your hearts and
minds.
May this manifestation lead you out of ignorance into the
Light.

Message No. 45

October 3, 1978

My dear friends, I am happy indeed to be with you once again and to speak to you in this way.

My Presence is being felt throughout the world.
My energy of Love, My Gift, creates among men a pool of happiness.
Dip deeply therein, My friends, and, shining with the Light of Love, emerge into a New Day.

My Masters are working to trace for you the outlines of the future.
Bear these well in mind.
The rock upon which that glorious future will be built is Love, Justice and Sharing.
Make it your aim, My friends, to link yourselves with those for whom these aspects are divine.
Create between you a wall of Light against which the world will knock in vain.

My Army moves.
My Lieutenants know the result of the battle and know the Plan of Action.
That action involves you all, for through you, My friends and brothers, must the New World be made.
Take then your part in this valiant work and show your mettle.
My Love will sustain you.
My Law will guide you.
My heart enfolds you always.
My friends, be not afraid — you have nothing to fear but your fear.

May the Divine Light and Love and Power of the One Most Holy God be now manifest within your hearts and minds.

May this manifestation lead you into the battle, and, with your brothers, to victory.

Message No. 46

October 10, 1978

My dear friends, I am happy to be with you once more.

My friends, I am happy, too, to tell you that My work
proceeds to plan.
All goes well, and soon My face and voice shall become
known to you.
May this manifestation release in you that aspiration
which I know shines ever in your heart.
May it be that you will accept Me and work closely with
Me for your brothers.
My major need today is for those who share My vision to
accept the responsibility of action.
Many millions there are in the world who know the need
of man, who see that vision, but know not the urgency of
the time.
I rely on all those with a knowledge of your brothers'
needs, a sympathy for the sufferings of so many, and a
will to change all that.
May you be among those upon whom I may call, that
together we can usher in a new and better world.

My heart responds to the tremor of your aspiration.
My Love kindles that fire.
My friends, fan that into a blaze and come with Me.
Hold fast to your vision of what may be, and reveal the
God within you all.

May the Divine Light and Love and Power of the One Most Holy God be now manifest within your hearts and minds.
May this manifestation lead you to be ever mindful of your identity with God.

Message No. 47

October 24, 1978

My dear friends, once again I am with you and happy I
am to be so.

Many are the ways in which you may recognise Me.
Look for Me, My friends, as a Teacher of men, outlining
the possibilities of the New Time.
Remember that I am a Man among men as well as a true
Son of God.
My Masters, too, are simple Men and come to live among
you as such.
Nothing separates Us from you; we shall live and work
among you as Brothers.
Remember this and look not for Gods.

My Teachings will be simple indeed, will show you the
way to God through Love and service to man.
My Plans are proceeding well and soon My face will
become known to you.
May it be that you will allow Me to guide you into the
future.

Very many now await My Presence.
Throughout the world men stand ready and poised for My
Appearance, knowingly or not.
When enough are so prepared, My Teaching will
penetrate their hearts and in Joy and Love will they
follow Me.
My heart knows this and makes light My Task.

May you be among the first of those who draw around
Me, through whom I may work and who in this way can
best serve their brothers.
My love for you knows no end.

May the Divine Light and Love and Power of the One
Most Holy God be now manifest within your hearts and
minds.
May this manifestation lead you to be enlightened from
your own True Self.

Message No. 48

October 31, 1978

I am with you once more, My dear friends.

It is part of My Plan to reveal Myself gradually, step by step to make My Presence known to the world.
This process is now well under way.
When you see Me, you will find a Friend in need, a Brother Whose heart enfolds your own, a Teacher Who has traveled somewhat further along the journey of life, a Guide into that blessed future which, My friends, will be yours.

My methods, simple as they are, are proving effective.
Witness for yourselves the changes occurring in the world.

My Entreaty is this: make yourself responsible for the spreading of the news of My Presence and do for Me a great work.
When your brothers know that I am with you, they will gladly accept your news.
Do this for Me, My friends.
Do this now.
Share with your brothers and sisters everywhere this message of Hope, these tidings of Joy, and prepare them, too, for My Appearance.
In this way can you serve your brothers beyond measure.

I am taking you into a New Country.
Close your ranks around Me and allow Me to show you the glories which await you.
The framework of this future time is now constructed.
The blueprint of the future becomes clearer.

Let Me take you with Me into that future and clothe in
radiant Light that structure.
My Blessings go with you all.

May the Divine Light and Love and Power of the One
Most Holy God be now manifest within your hearts and
minds.
May this manifestation lead you to see yourselves as the
Divine and glorious Beings that you are.

Message No. 49

November 7, 1978

My dear friends, I am happy indeed to be with you once
more and to tell you that My face will soon be known.

Your brothers support Me, give Me their trust and their
love, a love which I cherish.
So shall it be with you, My friends, when we meet
together.

Soon you will see the manifestation of a great change in
the world.
That change is wrought by My Energies and Presence.
Have no fear, all is well and proceeds to plan.

My Brothers, the Masters of Wisdom, will lead you
forward into the light of that Wisdom which is Theirs,
will unfold for you the panorama of man's past, will teach
you the ancient Laws and guide your feet into the future.
Look to Them as to an Elder Brother and, trusting, let
Them show you the Lighted Way.

My Plans unfold.
My heart embraces all who know Me, who come to Me
for help.
Thus shall it always be.
My brothers and sisters, My help is yours to command:
you have only to ask.
Take My hand, My friends, and let Me take you with Me
into your glory.

My Mission begins.

Already, much is accomplished.

Soon the tide will turn and men will sense and respond in joy to My Presence.

Make it your task to tell the others that I am among you.

Lead them, too, into the light.

Allow them to share with you this realisation and give to them the hope they need.

In this way, My friends, you will serve Me more than you could know.

May the Divine Light and Love and Power of the One Most Holy God be now manifest within your hearts and minds.

May this manifestation bring you into the realisation of your true nature as messengers of God.

Message No. 50

November 15, 1978

My dear friends, I am happy indeed to be with you once
more.

My Mission proceeds, My Plans evolve correctly.
Very little time now will elapse until you see My face.
Know it as the face of your Friend and Brother, come
once again to help you.
Take Me to your hearts as I, My dear brothers and sisters,
have taken you to mine, and, working together, let us
remake the world.
Let us change all that is corrupt and useless in your
structures, all that prevents the manifestation of your
divinity.
Let us together show the way for the little ones and hold
fast the world for them.
I appeal to you to aid Me in My task of succour.
Help Me to help the world, and fulfil this life.

My Coming is planned, is lawful and releases to you the
Love and Will of God.
I am the Manifestation of both Love and Will.
I am the Caretaker.
I am the One sent to teach you.
I am the Flute Player.

Many times before have I been among you.
Many times before have you given Me your love.
Once again, My friends, demonstrate your allegiance and
work with Me.

I am the Lawgiver.
I hear all pleas.
I come to save.
I render service.

Make yourselves one with Me and let us together serve
the Plan.

My Masters, too, are with you.
Let Them guide you into the future.
Make haste to recognise Me.
Make haste to serve Me.
Your brothers call both Me and you.
My people heed Me.
Join them, and manifest That which I am through you.

May the Divine Light and Love and Power of the One
Most Holy God be now manifest within your hearts and
minds.
May this Light and Love and Power lead to the
manifestation of that Divine Being Whom in truth you are.

Message No. 51

November 23, 1978

My dear friends, I am with you once more.

My Mission, as I have said, is twofold:
to release you from the bondage of your self-imposed
limitations, and to take you with Me back to God.
I shall show you that through the right distribution of this
Earth's manifold resources, all men may enjoy God's
bounty.
I shall show you, too, that the Path to God is simple
indeed, that your Divine Spark will become manifest
through Me.

Let Me do this work for you, My friends.
Let Me lead you into your divine heritage.
I shall show you wonders of which you cannot dream.
I shall release from your eyes the blindfold of ignorance.
I shall drive from this Earth forever the curse of hatred,
the sin of separation.
Let Me take you with Me, My friends, back to your
Source, back to the cradle of your Being, and release in
you your Godhead.

My Masters will serve you, too, will teach you to live
together in true brotherhood, in justice and harmony.
Forget not, My brothers, that you are One, that the Father
of All has created you in His divine image, that through
you shines the same blessed light of Love and Truth.

The time is coming, My friends, when the Light of Truth
shall shine all around you, when man shall take his
brother to his heart and know him as himself.

Let Me lead you, My friends, into that blessed state.
Say yes to My Advent.
Say yea to My Coming, and be enfolded in the blessing
of My Love.

May the Divine Light and Love and Power of the One
Most Holy God be now manifest within your hearts and
minds.
May this manifestation lead you to see yourselves,
together, as children of the One Father.

Message No. 52

November 28, 1978

My dear friends, I am happy to be with you once more.

My Plans are achieving their effects, and many stand
today in wonder at the changes which arise.
Thus, quietly, do I affect the balance of the world.
My energies of Love and Will create a reservoir of Truth
from which all men may drink.
Keep open your heart to this Higher Stream and make
yourself a channel for Me.
I need many such.

The problems of mankind are real but solvable.
The solution lies within your grasp.
Take your brother's need as the measure for your action
and solve the problems of the world.
There is no other course.

Mankind today faces a dilemma of truth — to march with
Me into the future or forever to despair.
Place yourselves behind Me in My Task and allow Me to
take you on the Lighted Way.
My Masters will help you, and together in Freedom and
Trust shall all men receive the Blessings of God.

My Plans unfold, and soon, in full and physical fact, shall
you know Me and, trusting, follow Me.
Be not surprised if My words are familiar to you; many
times before have you heard the need for Love.
Nevertheless, many today stand naked of this divine
aspect and perish in millions.

Therefore, My friends, My words will resound in your ears:
"Love your brother; heed his need; give of your plenty and restore joy to the world."

May the Divine Light and Love and Power of the One Most Holy God be now manifest within your hearts and minds.
May this manifestation lead you to be ever mindful of your identity with your brothers and God.

Message No. 53

December 7, 1978

My dear friends, I am happy to be with you once more.

My methods meet with success.
My agents work correctly and well, and all proceeds
to plan.
My plan is to remain in My centre until My Declaration is
made.
Then My progression round the countries of the world
will begin, and all men shall see My face.
When I place Myself before you, I shall ask for your
allegiance, for your help in service to your brothers.
I know already those on whom I may count.

My task will be to take you on a journey into Truth, into
the Blessed Country of Love, and there to show you to
yourselves as God.
My Masters, likewise, will take you by the hand and lead
you to His divine feet.

Let us together show the world:
that the need for war is past;
that the instinct of man is to live and to love;
that hatred is begotten of separation;
that the Law of God lives in man and is fundamental to
his nature.
All of this shall I show you.
Work with Me and prove this to be true.

I am the Conveyor of God's Love,
I am the Administrator of God's Will.

The Light of God dwells in Me and that Light do I turn
on you.
Grow therein, My friends, and shine with the Glory of
God.

My plan is to reveal Myself in such a way that few
indeed will know not who I am.
Therefore, watch for My Presence.
Seek out My face and words and hearken quickly to them.

My Blessing goes with you all.

May the Divine Light and Love and Power of the One
Most Holy God be now manifest within your hearts and
minds.
May this manifestation lead you to be ever mindful of
your likeness to God.

Message No. 54

December 14, 1978

My dear friends, I am happy to be with you once more
and to share with you My thoughts for man's future.

Man has far to go, for man stems from the highest Source.
Within all men sits a God.
That God is your true Self.
My task will be to release in you that Divine Being, and
so complete a Divine Plan.

There is nothing more simple than God, for behind all
things rests that divine principle.
When man sees this he will come into his true greatness,
and from him then will flow a creative stream.
My plan is to show you, step by step, the way to manifest
that divine principle and thus lead you to your Source.
If men accept Me they shall come into the truth of their
Godhead, and in the shining raiment of that Truth shall
stand revealed as God.
That Promise I do solemnly make.

Help Me, My friends, to do this work for you.
Reveal, now, the Spirit of God which already shines
within you, and together in Truth let us remake this world.

May the Divine Light and Love and Power of the One Most Holy God be now manifest within your hearts and minds.

May this manifestation lead you to stand revealed as the Gods you are.

Message No. 55

December 19, 1978

My dear friends, I am happy to be with you once more
and to add My glad tidings to this joyous festival.

My friends, I am with you here tonight in a certain
fashion, but soon you shall become aware that I, Maitreya
Himself, your Eldest Brother, am among you.
When you see Me you shall know that the turning point
has been reached, that My Forces are gathered in strength,
and that victory is assured.

My plan is to release into the world My simple Teaching
of truth:
that men are One, brothers all;
that God loves all men equally;
that nature provides the sustenance for everyone to share;
that, coming as I do from mankind's past,
I know the answers to man's dilemma.
I shall show you the simple ways of change, of correctly
relating one to another, of correctly manifesting the Will
of God.

My plan is to show you this and release you from your
limitations.
The way ahead is not easy, My friends, but with your
help, all shall be made good for mankind.

Take heart, My dear friends, from these words, and be
assured of My help and strength.

May the Divine Light and Love and Power of the One
Most Holy God be now manifest within your hearts and
minds.

May this manifestation lead you to sense the need of your
brother, and, sensing that, to render service to him.

Message No. 56

January 9, 1979

My dear friends, I am happy to be so close to you once more.

My friends, I am with you today in such a way to remind you of My Presence, and also of your task in the weeks and months ahead.

Many there are now in every corner of the world who sense that I am here; who study events and draw conclusions; who see the changes which daily mount in potency, and read the signs manifest in the world.

But many still are blind to the reality of My Presence among you, and this state would I gladly have you remedy.

Teach your brothers the truth of My Coming, the truth of My Departure so long ago, and the Promise which I now bring.

Tell them that Maitreya, their Brother, the Eldest of such, is with them once more.

Tell them that soon, for themselves, they will see Me and hear My words, and rejoice in My Presence.

Tell them that I come to teach the simple Laws of God, to teach men to share, to lead them into the Light of Truth, and to establish among them a vast network of Divine Light.

You, My friends, can aid Me in this task.

Take your place at My side.

Lead your brothers into that Light, and show that for all men exists a future bedecked in the Glory of God, a future vouchsafed to all men.

114

Tell your brothers this, My friends, and make way in their hearts for My Light and Love.
Prepare the ground before My feet.
Sustain My Task, and help yourselves to Bliss.

May the Divine Light and Love and Power of the One Most Holy God be now manifest within your hearts and minds.
May this manifestation lead you to be ever open to the influence of the agents of God.

Message No. 57

January 16, 1979

My dear friends, I am happy to be with you once more.

With the year 1979 begins a new phase of mankind's life.
My Presence is producing such changes that no one but
the most blind will, shortly, deny My Existence among
you.

My work proceeds smoothly and well, and all aspects of
My Plan are being fulfilled.
Nevertheless, there still is much to do, and I would set
you, therefore, this task:
tell men everywhere that you believe that the Teacher for
mankind is among them.
Tell them what you know of My plans and projects, and
illumine their lives.
Send My Words throughout the world and reach the
hearts of your brothers.
Help them, too, to share in a great manifestation of God's
Love, and awaken them to the promise of the future.
Do this for Me, My friends, and you will do a deed of
which forever you may be proud.

The central point of My Plan is to evoke in men the
desire to share, for on this principle all else rests.

Sharing, My friends, is an attribute of God.
To become the Gods which you are, this principle must
govern your lives.
Allow Me to remind you of this simple truth once again,
and show you the path to the future.
My Blessing goes with you all.

May the Divine Light and Love and Power of the One
Most Holy God be now manifest within your hearts and
minds.
May this manifestation allow you to teach the truth to all
you meet.

Message No. 58

January 23, 1979

My dear friends, I am happy indeed to be with you once more.

My Law is beginning to be fulfilled.
The ways of man are changing.
This I see more clearly, perhaps, than you can, but, if you will believe Me, it is so.

All that I say tonight pertains to the creation of a new living structure for mankind.
A new civilisation must be built on the ruins of the old.
That which is precious and worth preserving will be so preserved, but all that hinders the manifestation of man's true greatness must be discarded.
A time is coming, My friends, when you will see around you cities of beauty, glowing creations of Love, and all the manifestation of man's dreams of himself as God.
Thus will it be.

Many are the ways to perfection, but the simple ways are best.
My way, the Way of Love, will take man quickest to his Source.
If you can see this, you will proceed on a Path unerring and true, and for all men this is so.

When you see Me, you will know that the time has come to begin this work of change, of building the new, creating forms and structures which will reveal yourselves to each other as the Gods you are.
My Masters will help you in this work and I shall lead.

My plan is that you should see Me soon.

With your help this may be so.

I require the creation of a certain trust, an expectancy and hope.

In this way no force need be used.

My Law forbids such force.

Therefore, My friends, the task is yours to grasp.

Make known the fact that I am among you and create the climate in which shortly I may be seen.

That will not be as difficult as you might think, for mankind today stands on the verge of a revelation of its true nature and worth.

My Presence among you makes this so.

Your brothers will thank you for the work you do.

My Blessing goes with you all.

May the Divine Light and Love and Power of the One Most Holy God be now manifest within your hearts and minds.

May this manifestation lead you into the true sense of yourselves as My messengers.

Message No. 59

January 30, 1979

My brothers and sisters, happy I am to be among you
once more, and to reveal to you My intentions and plans.

My dear friends, I am about to appear among men in an
altogether new and more potent guise.
Many who see Me now wonder in their hearts from
whence I come.
Many see in Me their hopes and dreams fulfilled.
My Love penetrates their hearts and joyfully they give Me
their allegiance.
On a wider scale, also, will this be true, for, when men
see Me as I am, they will love Me and hearken to My
words.
Have no fear: men will follow Me for the love in their
hearts for their brothers, for it is for all men everywhere
that I shall speak.

Know Me by the simplicity of My utterance.
Know Me by the Love of My heart,
by My deeds of succour,
by My Call to all men to share and live in peace.
Know Me thus, My friends, and give Me your help.
I need not only your faith, but your willingness to work
for the unfoldment of God's Plan.
That Holy Plan shall I unfold for you, and together in
Love shall we see it fulfilled.

My plan is to come before the world so quickly now that
nothing which prevents your participation in this work
should be allowed to hinder.

Make it your primary task to acquaint your brothers and sisters throughout the world with the fact of My Presence, and create in them the joy you know.

My task will be to speak as the mouthpiece for all men everywhere;

to voice for them their hopes and desires for a better and saner life,

for the re-organisation of those structures which prevent the manifestation of the true divinity of man.

That is My Task, My dear friends, and that task lightly, and gladly, do I shoulder.

With your help, it will be achieved. Goodnight, My dear friends.

May the Divine Light and Love and Power of the One Most Holy God be now manifest within each and every one, whose Inner Light I now see.

Message No. 60

February 6, 1979

My dear friends, I am happy to be among you once more
in this fashion.

My dear ones, My Entreaty is this:
make known the fact of My Presence among men and
become responsible for the speed of My Emergence.
My task is to take you through the Gates of Initiation, to
lead you upward to the Light and back to the Source from
which you come.
My intention is to proceed at once on My way, to bring
you, those who are ready, before the Father, and to show
you His face.

I would have you know that much depends on you,
depends on your ability to create the necessary hope and
expectation for My Appearance.
I rely on you to do this work for Me and so serve your
brothers and Me.

I came before as a Man misunderstood and rejected by
many.
I return today, not to conquer but to lead;
to show men their true nature as sons of God;
to show men that they have come from a high place
indeed, and thus have far to go.

I am the Means and the Way.
I am the Fruit of God's Labours.
I build the Temple of Love.
I accept those who are ready.
I love all men.

Take That which I am into your Being and reveal the God within.

I know God's Plan.
I teach all men.
I reveal the Truth.
I bring a New Light.
I create the New World through men.
I am the Beginning and the End.
I am the Love of God.
I am the Soul of Creation.
I am God made Flesh.
I am All Things.

I am your Heart.
I am your Delight.
I am your Purpose.
I am vouchsafed to you.

May the Divine Light and Love and Power of the One Most Holy God be now manifest within your hearts and minds.
May this manifestation clear from your eyes the blindfold of ignorance.

Message No. 61

February 14, 1979

My dear friends, I am happy indeed to be among you
once more in this way, and to release to you something of
My Plans.

Within the group wherein I dwell are those who know Me
for what I am, but it is My intention to withhold for a
certain time My true status.
This will enable you to see Me as One of yourselves, a
Man among men.
Nothing which I do will seem extraordinary.
Nothing which I say will be bizarre or strange.
Simple indeed will be My approach.
On this fact you may count.

As a Brother among brothers I shall speak for you all,
voice aloud your aspirations and hopes;
make known the desire of all men for a world at peace,
for a just and noble readiness to share,
for the creation of a society based on freedom and love.
By My enunciation of these principles will you know and
discover Me.

My intention is to reveal Myself soon and by the shortest
route.
All else failing, I shall emerge into a world ready but
unprepared, a world which knows not yet that I am
among you.

But far better would it be for Me to come before you as
the Expected One, the One sent by God to lead you into
your future glory.

Many know this, but many more by far are ignorant of the true happenings of the time.

I do solemnly appeal to you, therefore, My dear friends, to make known the fact of My Presence among you and pave smooth My way.

My burdens are heavy indeed.
These burdens may be lightened by your work. I trust you to act and follow.
Together we shall complete the Plan.

My Blessings go with you all.

May the Divine Light and Love and Power of the One Most Holy God be now manifest within your hearts and minds.
May this manifestation lead you to be ever mindful of your true purpose as servants of the Plan.

Message No. 62

February 21, 1979

My dear friends, I am happy indeed to be among you
once more.

My happy ones, My glad ones, I see within you now the
glow of the Light of Truth, the truth of My Presence
among you.
That Light shall I fan into a blaze of glory in this coming
blessed time.

My Masters, too, are among you and will show you the
way to manifest your divine gifts, those which lie
dormant within your hearts.
My friends, I am nearer to you than you could know, for I
sit within the heart of all those who love their brothers, of
all those who wish to share and release the light of Justice
and Freedom into the world.

I am within you now.
I see Myself, That which I am, within the lotus of your
hearts, arrayed in the colours of your aspiration, and from
this do I derive great joy.
It is that Light within you which has brought Me to you.
Let it manifest abroad in all its power and glory and light
a pathway for Me in the world.

My task is to bring you, My friends, before the Father,
before the Gilded Throne of the Shining One, there to
present you to Him and establish you within Our Ranks.

My Prophecy holds: I shall take before the Father all who are ready in this coming time.
That is the Task given to Me by Him Whom we together serve.

My aim is to present Myself to the world in such a fashion that no-one will mistake Me for other than I am.
May you be alert and awake, see Me quickly, draw yourself and others around Me, and let Me work through you.

My dear ones, I have need of all those who are ready for sacrifice, the simple giving of themselves in love for their brothers.
Do this for Me and for them, and restore in the world the Ways of God.
My Blessing goes with you all.

May the Divine Light and Love and Power of the One Most Holy God be now manifest within your hearts and minds.
May this manifestation lead you to express That which I am.

Message No. 63

February 28, 1979

My dear friends, I am happy indeed to be among you
once more in this way.

My friends and brothers, I am happy, also, to tell you that
My Emergence into full and public vision has commenced.
For yourselves, soon, therefore, will you see that the
Prince of Peace has returned;
that your Brother of Old, once again, walks among men;
that the Preacher has returned in a new guise, but is
essentially the Representative of God.

When you see Me you will know, My friends,
that the New Time indeed has begun: the time of building
the new signposts to the future;
the time to establish among all peoples correct
relationship and trust;
to advance together in Harmony and Sharing, lighting a
path for those who will follow.

When you see Me, you will know this.
You will know, also, that I come, not as a God
omnipotent to rule, but simply, as an Elder Brother, to
show you the way.
When you have grasped My intention, you will see that
that way leads directly to God, for it is the Way planned
for you from the beginning.
No man, throughout the history of the world, has come to
his Source by another route.

My friends, brothers and children, know this to be true
and follow Me.

Follow My footsteps into the Light of the future which today beckons all men.

Let Me lead you therein, and, clasped together in Love, make salutations to the Father of All.

With His help, this will be so.

My intention is to show Myself more openly so soon now that little time indeed remains to inform your brothers of My Presence.

Go to, with a will, My friends: make known your belief in My Return among you, and light within the hearts of all the Light of Truth.

May the Divine Light and Love and Power of the One Most Holy God be now manifest within your hearts and minds.

May this manifestation lead you to be ever imbued with the truth of the Spirit of God.

Message No. 64

March 6, 1979

My dear friends, I am happy to be among you once more.

My Emergence proceeds. My face is known to a growing body of men in the centre of My choice, and soon many of you, for yourselves, will know that I am here.

My message tonight is this: prepare all those who know not yet that I have returned for My Presence among them. Release in them the hope which My Return creates and do for Me and them a service untold.
My need is great for those who see the promise and the dangers of the time.
I trust you, My brothers and sisters,
to work for Me in this way,
to lift from the world the peril of war,
to relieve the hunger of many,
and to restore well-being to the world.

My Teaching, simple though it is, will show you the necessity for sharing, for the creation of a pool of resources from which all men may take, the substitution for greed of co-operation and trust, the manifestation of the inner divinity of men.
This manifestation, My friends, must proceed, for without it, the future for man would be black indeed.
A crisis of decision awaits mankind.
My Love creates a polarity of viewpoints; that is the Sword which I wield.
My friends, know well where you stand and receive My Light.

Take care where you place your feet: on the steps which
lead to tomorrow or — oblivion.

Men and women of the world, My brothers, My children,
I appeal to you: take the upward path into the light of the
Truth which I bring, and be enabled to manifest the Gods
which you are.

Many there are now who know this to be the only path
for man.

Make it known where you, My friends, stand at this time.

My Blessings go with you all.

May the Divine Light and Love and Power of the
Everlasting God be now manifest within your hearts and
minds.

May this manifestation lead you into the expression of
your true nature as luminous Gods.

Message No. 65

March 13, 1979

My dear friends, I am happy indeed to be with you once more, to tell you something of My plans and of how they will affect you in this coming time.

My plan is to emerge quickly, and, maintaining a certain rhythm, make known My Presence to the world.
In My centre, steps have already been taken which have allowed many of your brothers and sisters to see My face, hear My words, respond to My Presence and Call to Action.
Great, indeed, has been the enthusiasm of your brothers, which bodes well for the future of My Mission.
When you, yourselves, see Me, you will, I feel sure, respond likewise, for within you all does sit the same Light of Truth, of Justice and Freedom which I awaken in all who hear Me.
Therefore, My friends, have no fear that mankind will reject Me.
My Plans are safe in your hands.

My Coming will transform this world, but the major work of restoration must be done by you.
I am the Architect, only, of the Plan.
You, My friends and brothers, are the willing builders of the Shining Temple of Truth.
I shall give you the Key of that Temple, and entering therein shall you know God.

My Masters await, also, your response to Their guidance.
Give Them your trust and let Them lead you into the
New Dawn, sharing together the Earth's produce,
knowing together the joy of Brotherhood, manifesting
together the divinity within you all.

The time is short indeed till you shall see Me.
Make best use of this little time to prepare My way, to
teach all those whom you meet with the words of Truth
which I send to you.
Lead them, too, into the Path of Light and the Promise
which My Return brings to the world.
My Emergence in full vision is imminent.
Watch and wait and sleep not.

May the Divine Light and Love and Power of the One
Most Holy God be now manifest within your hearts and
minds.
May this manifestation lead you to seek and to find that
Essential Being Whom always you have been.

Message No. 66

March 20, 1979

My dear friends, I am happy indeed to be with you once more in this way.

My Mission proceeds; all that I hope for is being achieved, and augurs well for the future.
My plan is to present Myself to the people of the world within so short a time that few indeed will doubt My Presence.
My words will teach you the Ways of God, the way forward into the blessed future which I see before you.
Into the light of the highest dreams of man shall I take you.
The Path of Brotherhood will vouchsafe this for you.

My plan is to realise within you that which you truly are, to show you that you stem from the Godhead Itself, and to that Divine Source must return.
My Mission will ease for you that passage, that long journey back to your rightful heritage.
When we meet as brothers, My friends, you will find in Me a Teacher and Guide Who knows well the way, for long since have I made that self-same journey, and know by heart the signposts on the way.

Make sure that you miss Me not.
Look well, My friends, for My appearance may surprise you.

As a simple Man, indeed, am I now among you, teaching My friends and brothers on the way, releasing to them My Gifts of Love, Wisdom and

Joy, gathering them to Me as brothers in work.

You, likewise, My dear friends, can rest in the knowledge that your work for Me and for your brothers is welcome indeed.

I need you all, all who will take upon themselves the burden of service to the world, to create anew this shining world out of the chaos of the past.

My Blessings go with you all.

May the Divine Light and Love and Power of the One Most Holy God be now manifest within your hearts and minds.

May this manifestation lead you to see yourselves as My co-workers, brothers in Light. ˙

Message No. 67

April 18, 1979

My dear friends, once again I have the pleasure of speaking to you in this way.

My pleasure is doubled in that I see among you so many in whom the Light of Truth shines forth.
Great is the joy which this affords Me.

My friends, My brothers and sisters, all proceeds to plan.
Today there is in this world the fulfilment of the Prophecies of Old.
My Presence is a fact.
My Love abounds.
My Creative Will plans your future glory.
The tendency today is to reject that which is simple, to cling to the complex, the erudite and vague; but all that pertains to Truth, My friends, will be found to be simple indeed.
Thus am I a simple Man.
When you see Me you will know this, and smilingly take Me as a Brother.

Many there are who fear My Advent.
The guilt of ages sits upon their shoulders and they trust not.
My friends, through Me shall be created the Era of Trust, the removal of guilt, the Citadel of Love.

In awe do men await Me.
My friends, I am not God.
As your Brother, your Friend, your Teacher, do I come.
Forget this not.

My plans unfold, My way is being cleared.
There are growing around Me now those who recognise
Me as the spirit of the New Time.
They give Me their trust and allegiance, and I speak for
them.
When you see Me, My friends and brothers, you, too, can
join this band of workers, this Company of Light, and
make manifest the God within.

The time has come for sight and sound of Truth.
I answer the call.
My Mission will restore to men the vision of God.
Take your place at My side and let Me show you that
vision.

May the Divine Light and Love and Power of the One
Most Holy God fall now upon the hearts and minds of all.
Through this manifestation may you come quickly to My
side.

Message No. 68

May 4, 1979

I am with you once more, my dear friends.

Tonight I would like to tell you that My Mission proceeds
as planned.
My heart enfolds all those who await My Coming and, in
trust, expect Me.
My Light, which within them shines, has brought them to
this realisation.
In this way do I make known My Advent.

You, My friends, have a unique opportunity to serve at
this time.
You are in receipt of a message of Hope, a declaration of
Truth, and on your judgment rests your future.
You may take the path that leads to sterile inaction —
that is your right.
But, My friends, why discard an opportunity to serve your
brothers and Me in a most potent fashion?
Make known the fact of My Presence among you and see
the Light of Joy awaken in your brothers' eyes.
Let them, too, share in this manifestation of Hope and
Promise for the world and take your place by My side.

Soon you will see Me.
Soon you will know that the One for Whom the world
has waited has arrived, has returned to serve, to lead man,
if he wills, into a new and blessed time.

My thanks go to those who already work for My Cause.
Make yourselves one with those valiant ones and share in
this Holy Work.

There is no need to fear. My plans unfold and soon the demonstration of peace shall enfold the world.

Man's way is clear. Behind mankind today stand their Brothers of Old, their Guides and Leaders, their Elder Brothers.

Under Their wise guidance, mankind shall know the Peace of God.

May the Divine Light and Love and Power of the One Most Holy God be now manifest within your hearts and minds.

May this manifestation lead you in Light to the feet of God.

Message No. 69

May 9, 1979

My dear friends, I am happy indeed to be among you once more, and to see shining from you the light of Truth.

The key to My Teaching rests, as you know, on the principle of Sharing.
All that men do and all that man will do depends on this simple and basic truth:
that from the One we call God flows the Providence for all men.
Accept this as a fact, My friends, and enter your divinity.
Within you all sits such a God, and through men, together, can that God manifest.
This is the way planned for you from the beginning.
When men see this, they will know the truth of Brotherhood.

My Mission proceeds and steadily My face and voice become known.
Your brothers accept that a new Teacher is among them and will show them the Path to the future.
Likewise, when you see Me, My brothers and friends, you will join with Me in a great manifestation of God's Love and create in the world a new Truth, a new Light, a new and shining City of Love.
My task is to lead you therein and perform for you the requirements of God.
I guard the Gates through which all pass to Him.

If you would serve Me and serve the world, make known, My friends, that I am here.

In this way can you build the sure wall of Hope against which the tide of fear will beat in vain.
My Blessings go with you all.

May the Divine Light and Love and Power of the One Most Holy God be now manifest within your hearts and minds.
May this manifestation lead you to see yourselves as My disciples and helpers.

Message No. 70

May 17, 1979

Good evening, My dear friends. Once again, I am happy to be among you in this way.

My Plan proceeds carefully and well.
Your brothers grow in number around Me and to them do I give My Blessing and Teaching.
Likewise, in due course, shall I bestow on you these Gifts.
My aim is to spread abroad My net to the widest horizon, to draw to Me all those in whom My Light shines, that through them I may work.
This cast can include you, My friends, for I need all who share with Me the desire to serve the world.
Take upon yourselves the task of succour and share My burden.
Share with Me, My friends, in a Great Work — nothing less than the transformation of this world.

My means, as you know, are simple.
I need no other tools than the heart's love of man.
This, My friends, bestowed on you by That from which you come, will bring men to the Source of Love Itself.
Make it manifest, My brothers, and join Our Ranks.

I am the Custodian of the Plan of God.
I am the New Direction.
I am the Way for all men.
I hold the Secrets of Old.
I bestow Bliss.
I create the desire for Truth.
I make all men One.
I come to realise My Truth through men.

I am the Saviour of Old.
I am the Teacher of the New.
I am the Guide for the Future Time.
I am the Law embodied.
I am Truth Itself.
I am your Friend and Brother.
I am your Self.

Take within you That which I am and make That manifest in the world.

Take within you That which I bestow and create the City of Light.

Manifest around you That which I pronounce and become as Gods.

May the Divine Light and Love and Power of the One Most Holy God be now manifest within your hearts and minds.
May this manifestation lead you to be encircled by the Aura of God.

Message No. 71

June 5, 1979

My dear friends, I am happy indeed to be among you once more in this way.

My Teaching goes forth.
Your brothers respond and bring joy to My heart.
When you see Me, you, too, will share in this manifestation of God's Love, for I am but the Spokesman for the One Who sent Me.

My Teaching will show you that there is nothing in this world which, if needed, cannot be achieved by man.
Man is a God and requires only to manifest that divinity to flourish.
My Presence will assure you that this is so, for My Brothers, the Masters of Wisdom, and I shall show you the wonders of your divine nature.
In this way shall you sense your potential and grow in Light.

My friends, I am among you in this way to ask you to help Me, to release to your brothers and sisters the truth of My Presence, the fact of My Return.
Let them share in the beauty that this Promise brings, and lead them to Me.

My Task unfolds. My work proceeds, and soon in full vision shall you see and know Me.
My task will be to take you into the Light of your own true nature, and realise for you the Gods you are.

My task can be lightened, My path shortened, by your work.

Let Me ask you, My friends, to do this for Me, and show your love for your brothers.

Many are the ways to serve.

Choose that which suits you best and serve, My friends.

Through this act of service will you know God.

May the Divine Light and Love and Power of the One Most Holy God be now manifest within your hearts and minds.

May this manifestation lead you into service for your brothers.

Message No. 72

June 12, 1979

I am with you once again, My dear friends, and I am happy to be so.

My Forces are gathering around Me.
My Army strengthens from day to day, and in planned and full array will it march into the light, that New Light which I bring to the world.
Listen well, My friends, and you will hear the jingle of the harness of My Troops.
Listen well, My friends, and respond to the thunder of their drums.
My Call goes forth. I summon all who would go with Me.
I am among you, My friends, in such a way to call you, too, to My side.
Take your places, My brothers, in this Company of Light, and share the joy of the creation of a New World.

My task is simple: to lead you into a battle for Life.
My aim is vast: to release to you that Life in abundance.

Have no fear, My friends: the result of that battle is known to Me.
My Mission proceeds in such a fashion that victory now is assured.
Let Me lead you then, My friends, into your heritage, into your true nature as sons of God.

My Masters are now returning ahead of schedule.
This will allow Them, too, to share in this great and final battle for the world.

We are behind you, My Brothers and I.
We know the Way.
We send you Our Strength.
Take within you this Armour and show your valour.

The days are numbered when you will see My face.
Look for the face of a Friend and Guide.

May the Divine Light and Love and Power of the One
Most Holy God be now manifest within your hearts and
minds.
May this manifestation lead you to your places in Our
Ranks.

Message No. 73

June 19, 1979

My dear ones, it is with joy that I take this further
opportunity to speak to you in this manner.

My joy likewise is enlarged when I see within you the
Spirit of Love manifesting.
This brings to My heart a joy which you cannot know.
Men think of Myself and My Brothers in isolation.
This, My friends, is far from the truth.
Each tremor of Love felt within your heart is registered in
mine.
This is the simple truth of our relationship.
Know then, My friends, how great is the joy I feel when I
sense your expectation, your release from fear, and know
your trust.

My way is being prepared.
Make it your task, My brothers and sisters, to share this
burden.
Create around you the atmosphere of trust and hope into
which I soon may enter.
Believe Me, My friends, this is a Great Work indeed.
Much depends on the creation of this pool of Trust, this
atmosphere of hope.

When I tell you that My feet have already walked the
pavements of your cities, this, My friends, is the truth.
Men are known to Me in the fullest sense:
I know their hopes and fears.
I know their longings and yearnings.
I know their aspiration for good.
Upon all of this I rely.

Make it your avowed task to aid Me in My coming work.
May it be that you become channels for My Love.
In this way shall you fulfil your destiny, too.

May true Divine Light and Love and Power of the One
Most Holy God be now manifest within your hearts and
minds.
May this manifestation lead you to see yourselves as My
agents.

Message No. 74

July 3, 1979

Good evening, My dear friends.

I have come once more in this way to tell you that My Mission proceeds as planned.

Naught hinders the progress of this Holy Work, and soon, for yourselves, you will see the fruit of My efforts.

The time has come to begin the process of change, to transform the life of men in such a way that the God in man shines forth.

This, My friends, is not difficult of accomplishment for within you all sits such a Divine Being.

My task will be to evoke from you that Shining Light, and take you to Its Source.

My Masters work also in Their various centres and through Them proceeds the Plan.

My work is to organise that Plan in such a way that the least cleavage results.

Much that is loved must go.

Cling not to the old forms.

Much will depend on man's ability to renounce these outworn structures and to create a new and simpler world. Remember this.

Forget not that I come to change all things.

My Coming brings peace.

Likewise, My Presence brings cleavage.

My Sword, that Love which I am, will separate all men, will show the true from the false, will clear the way for the New Light which I bring.

May it be that you can withstand this change and accept
My Light.

Many times before have I told you that My Appearance is
nigh.
Look then carefully, My friends, and miss Me not.
My Blessing goes with you all.

May the Divine Light and Love and Power of the One
Most Holy God be now manifest within your hearts and
minds.
May this manifestation allow you quickly to hearken to
My Call.

Message No. 75

July 10, 1979

My dear friends, I am happy indeed to be among you
once more in this fashion.

I bring glad tidings.
With joy, I reveal that a further manifestation of Myself
to the public will shortly take place.
Many more, then, of your brothers and sisters will avail
themselves of this occurrence, and will see and hear Me.
The time when you yourselves may see Me is short,
therefore, indeed.

When you see Me, you will know that your Friend and
Brother of Old is with you once again, that your former
Teacher has returned to reveal to you a further page in the
great book of life.
By My counsel you will be enabled to transform those
institutions which require change.
By My example you will be inspired to reach upwards to
the Source of Life Itself.
By My Love you will be taken within the Temple of
Truth, and will see God.

My friends, My brothers, I am with you at last.
For long have I waited to bring to you the Light of the
future.
My Brothers and I look to this coming time as an
opportunity for Service.
We, too, My friends, grow by the manifestation of this
divine attribute.
Naught which stems from God but serves, My brothers.
Learn and believe that this is so.

Through service to man, man will come to God.
It was ever so.
Make a life of Service your vow for the future time and
know the bliss of the Love of God.

My Purpose unfolds.
My way clears.
My words are being heard.
My Love encircles all.

May the Divine Light and Love and Power of the One
Most Holy God be now manifest within your hearts and
minds.
May this manifestation lead you, in service, to the feet of
God.

Message No. 76

July 17, 1979

My dear friends and disciples, it is with pleasure that I
come among you once more in this way.

My heart leaps with joy when I see above and around you
the shining light of My Truth.
Keep it burnished well, My friends, and together we shall
work.

My Presence is evoking change.
My Law begins to be fulfilled.
My Masters return to the world, and the people wait in
expectation of revelation.
The New Truth which I bring will reveal to you an aspect
of God's nature which I, Myself, am.
Through My Presence, this nature will manifest through
those who are ready, and they, My brothers and sisters,
shall see the face of God.
Long ago I told you that God is Love.
Verily, this is so.
But that Love, My friends, flows from a higher Source
and That I shall reveal to you.

My plan is to come before the people stage by stage.
Those who would know Me must look for a simple Man
indeed, a Brother and a Friend, a Teacher and a Guide, a
Lover of God and men.
When you see Me, you will come to know the nature of
God as Light and Love and Will.
May it be that these divine aspects shall reflect through
you.
When this is so, I may work through you.

I need you.

I need you all to share with Me in the reconstruction of this world, to restore to men their faith and joy, to release the wherewithal to live to the needy of this Earth, and so restore balance.

My task is to show you the method; yours is to act and implement My Plan.

I know I can trust and call on you.

My Love embraces all.

May the Divine Light and Love and Power of the One Most Holy God be now manifest within your hearts and minds.

May this manifestation take you quickly, in joy, to your Source.

Message No. 77

July 26, 1979

My dear friends, I am happy indeed to be with you once more in this way.

My Emergence takes place in mounting rhythm.
My brothers and sisters, within a few days, shall see and hear Me.
I shall speak to them of the need for Love and Justice in the affairs of men, in the affairs of state, in the association of peoples; and I shall show them that without this Divine Love and Justice all men will perish.
My hope is — nay, My brothers, My knowledge is — that mankind will respond to My Call.
I know this to be so.
I know that within men sits a Divine Being, Whose Plan it is that Love and Justice should triumph.
This being so, the end is assured.

But not all see the necessity for change, for the transformation of this world, for the implementation of sharing, co-operation and trust.
When My simple Law, the Law of Love, is obeyed, all of this will ensue.
Therefore, My friends, I speak simply of Love and Trust.

Many today know that these aspects count, but realise not their central place.
My friends, all life depends for its existence on the Love of God.
This simple Truth I teach.
Make it your own.
Make it central to your lives, and advance with Me.

My Brothers, the Masters of Wisdom, will show you the
simple Path to the future, a future planned for you by the
One we call God.
That Path can be followed by all men, and through My
Agency shall they come to God.

We are with you, My Brothers and I.
We send you Hope.
We send you Courage.
We ask for your trust.
We need your allegiance.
We count on your divinity.

May the Divine Light and Love and Power of the One
Most Holy God be now manifest within your hearts and
minds.
May this manifestation lead you to see yourselves as My
colleagues and workers in the Light.

Message No. 78

August 2, 1979

My dear friends, I am happy indeed to be among you in this way and to tell you that My Plans unfold.

I have around Me now a group of brothers and sisters who see Me as their Leader and Guide to the future. To them do I speak of man's troubles, of man's imperfections, of man's need for change; but also I tell them that man is a God, a Divine Being of Light, Who one day shall stand arrayed as such.

The choice is man's alone.
If he chooses the Path which I shall indicate, that divinity shall verily shine forth.
Otherwise, My brothers and sisters, the future for man would be fateful indeed.

But, My friends, I know beforehand your answer and choice.
Through your love — the love in your heart for your brothers — have no fear, My dear ones: you will choose correctly.
This love will radiate throughout the world and on this you may count.
My Presence guarantees that this shall be so.
Already, the changes are occurring in such magnitude that victory is assured.

When you see Me, you will know that your Elder Brother has taken this step through Love of His brethren.
That, My friends, is why I am now among you.

But also you have called Me; your cry for help has reached My ears, and gladly do I answer that call.

May the coming time bring to you the knowledge of My Presence, the sight of My appearance, the sound of My words; and when you see Me and hear Me, hearken to Me. I need all those who long to serve, who wish to fulfil their purpose in life, who see this life as a step on the way, and accept the lever of Service as the greatest gift.
Make then your choice: to serve and follow Me, or relinquish progress.

I am with you always.

May the Divine Light and Love and Power of the One and Holy God be now manifest within your hearts and minds.
May this manifestation lead you in Light to My side.

Message No. 79

August 28, 1979

My dear friends, I am happy indeed to be with you once more in this fashion, and to tell you that My work proceeds well.

Already, many of your brothers in My centre have heard My words, have seen My face, and have responded to My Call.
Soon, for yourselves, you will know, and awaken to, the fact of My Presence.

When you see Me, you will know that the time for action has come, for I count on you, My friends, to act in implementing My Plan.
For many of you, this is an old and well-known mode of life; you are servers come to serve your brothers.
It is as such that I shall call on you, and I value highly your help.
Without that willing help, My Mission would be a burden indeed.

Now that I am among you, I have discovered even more keenly that mankind is ready to share.
Within all those who hear Me, I see the burning light of Justice and Truth.
I voice simply their desire, and thus evoke that Truth.
So will it be with you, My friends, for even as I speak I see shining within you this Divine Light.
Let it shine brightly forth, My dear friends, and show the way for your brothers.

160

My Coming is not without problems, for I do engender in all I meet a sense of a new and mysterious future.
This causes many to fear, but without cause, My friends. All should know that the future for all men, through My Presence, is bright indeed.
A new and wholesome Brotherhood will flourish among men, and the Justice of God shall be found arrayed in the Glory of God.
I come to teach you this.
I come to show you the way.
My friends, I count on you.

May the Divine Light and Love and Power of the One Most Holy God be now manifest within your hearts and minds.
May this manifestation lead you to see yourselves as brothers all.

Message No. 80

September 6, 1979

My dear friends, I am happy indeed to be with you once more in this fashion, and to tell you that My work in the world proceeds well.

All that I intend takes place.
All that I attempt succeeds.
When I make Myself known, you will know that the moment to inaugurate God's Plan has come.
This Plan, My dear friends, contains within it the future for all men and all things in the world.
With the help of man himself, that Plan will work out.
My Presence among you guarantees that this is so.

I embody the Plan of God.
I am the Benefactor.
I reach men through Love.
I teach men through Law.
I send Blessings to the world.
I engender Hope.
The City of Love will be built through Me.

The Masters of Wisdom, My Disciples, are Themselves among you; slowly They take Their places in Their centres.
When My name is known, Their names, likewise, shall be known.

My brothers and sisters, take within you That which I am, and prepare to see a New Light.
Hold within you That which I give, and know the meaning of Truth.

Release within you That which you eternally are, and become Gods.

I am among you now.
I see your dreams of Trust and Love.
I feel your aspiration and hopes.
I shall take these to My heart and accomplish them for you.

I am your Mentor.
I am your highest wish.
I am your clearest light.
I am your heart's love.

I shall take you to that Blessed Country which I call Love.
I shall show you God dwelling therein, and evoke from you that divinity.

Hold fast to your Truth.
Hold fast to your Light.
Hold fast, My friends, My brothers, to your Love.
Manifest that Love and follow Me.

May the Divine Light and Love and Power of the One Most Holy God be now manifest within your hearts and minds.
May this manifestation lead you to see yourselves as each other.

Message No. 81

September 12, 1979

My dear friends, I am happy indeed to be with you once more, and to magnetise your aspiration in this way.

My Coming evokes in man a desire for change, a desire for betterment, however expressed.
My Energies engender in man divine discontent.
All that is useless in our structures must go.
There are many such which are unworthy of man today.

Man is an emerging God and thus requires the formation of modes of living which will allow this God to flourish. How can you be content with the modes within which you now live: when millions starve and die in squalor; when the rich parade their wealth before the poor; when each man is his neighbour's enemy; when no man trusts his brother?
For how long must you live thus, My friends?
For how long can you support this degradation?

My plan and My duty is to reveal to you a new way, a way forward which will permit the divine in man to shine forth.
Thus do I speak gravely, My friends and brothers.
Hearken well to My words.
Man must change or die: there is no other course. When you see this you will gladly take up My Cause, and show that for man exists a future bathed in Light.

My Teaching is simple:
Justice, Sharing and Love are divine aspects.
To manifest his divinity, man must embrace these three.

May the Divine Light and Love and Power of the One Most Holy God be now manifest within your hearts and minds.
May this manifestation bring you to the realisation of your part in the Great Plan.

Message No. 82

September 18, 1979

My dear friends, I am happy indeed to be among you
once more in this fashion, and to set before you some
guidelines for the future.

My task will be to show you how to live together
peacefully as brothers.
This is simpler than you imagine, My friends, for it
requires only the acceptance of Sharing.
Sharing, indeed, is divine.
It underlies all progress for man.
By its means, My brothers and sisters, you can come into
correct relationship with God; and this, My friends,
underlies your lives.
When you share, you recognise God in your brother.
This is a truth, simple, but until now difficult for man to
grasp.
The time has come to evidence this truth.

By My Presence, the Law of Sharing will become
manifest.
By My Presence, man will grow to God.
By the Presence of Myself and My Brothers, the New
Country of Love shall be known.
Take, My friends, this simple Law to your hearts.
Manifest Love through Sharing, and change the world.
Create around you the atmosphere of peace and joy, and
with Me make all things new.

My Coming portends change;
likewise, grief at the loss of the old structures.

But, My friends, the old bottles must be broken — the
new wine deserves better.
My friends, My brothers, I am near you now.
I see above and around you your aspiration for Love and
Joy.
I know this to be widespread in mankind; this makes
possible My Return.

Let Me unveil for you your divine inheritance.
Let Me show you the wonders of God which yet
await you.
Allow Me to take you simply by the hand and lead you to
the Forest of Love,
the Glade of Peace,
the River of Truth.

Take My hand, My friends, and know this to be yours,
now.

May the Divine Light and Love and Power of the One
Most Holy God be now manifest within your hearts and
minds.
May this manifestation lead you in trust to the Country I
call Love.

Message No. 83

September 28, 1979

My dear friends and disciples, I am happy indeed to be
among you once more in this way.
My Plans unfold.
My brothers and sisters are awakening to My Presence
and for themselves chart a new course.
This is encouraging indeed, for, despite My Plans,
mankind's will is free.
When, therefore, I witness man's response, great is My
joy.

My Teaching is simple, as you know:
Love, Justice and correct Sharing are necessary for man
to live.
Those around Me now, in My centre, are learning this, are
responding to My Call and awakening to the promise of
the future.
For you too shall this be so, for within you now I see the
same divine intention.
Therefore, My friends, fear not for My Mission.
My plan is to come before the world so soon that only the
most abject mind will deny My Presence.
Great, even now, are the changes which occur:
the nations grow together in a new bond of harmony.
Witness for yourselves these events.
When My face is seen on a wider scale, this
transformation will gain a new impetus, and much,
quickly, will be achieved.

I trust you, My friends, to help Me in this work, to take your part in this Plan of God; for My Father has sent Me to show you the way to Him.
That Task do I lightly take up.

May the Divine Light and Love and Power of the One Most Holy God be now manifest within your hearts and minds.
May this manifestation prove to you the fact of My Advent.

Message No. 84

October 3, 1979

My dear friends, once again I am with you and am happy to be so close to you.

Many of My friends and disciples in the world know now that My Presence is an established fact, but many more by far are still ignorant of this blessed truth.
Therefore, My friends, My brothers, My disciples, it behoves you to work harder and thus make known on the widest scale that I am among you.
In doing this, you serve your brothers in a way second to none; at this time, nothing finer in Service can be achieved by you.
Therefore, My friends, the divinity within you, shining as always, exhorts you to this measure to aid My Cause.

Learn the Ways of God, My brothers, by following My Precepts.
My Teaching, simple as it is, will show you the straight path to the Source, and along that Shining Path are those Sentinels and Guardians Who know the way.
We, My Brothers and I, will show you that Way and, trusting, you will see God.
My way, the Way of Truth, of Light, of simple Brotherhood, is the Way for all men.
Each one among you can take this open path to God, and under My guidance come to know God.

Where, My friends, are the alternatives?
There is nowhere else to go.
All around you, God shines in Its Glory;
within you and around you shines this Blessed Truth.

170

The day is coming, My friends, when men everywhere
shall see this Truth and stand ablaze with the Glory of the
Divine Source.

Look not then for other ways to go, for
the Path is clear,
the steps of ascent are hewn,
the signposts are set,
the Guides are at hand;
the end is divinity itself.
Who, My friends, knowing this could accept less?

My Plans further unfold.
My face and words are seen and heard.
My Emergence proceeds apace, and soon the world will
know that their Teacher has come.
Make it your task, then, to make known these facts, this
Promise, and inherit your glory.

May the Divine Light and Love and Power of the One
Most Holy God be now manifest within your hearts and
minds.
May this manifestation lead you quickly to see and accept
your service.

Message No. 85

October 12, 1979

My friends, My dear ones, I am happy to be among you once more in this way.

My Plans progress. My face and words are known to many of your brothers and gradually My Presence becomes known.
Taking stock of My Mission thus far, I see changes so radical that My Plans unfold sooner than I anticipated.
This being so, My brothers, My face will become known to you before long.

When you see Me, My friends, know then that the hand of your Friend is yours to grasp;
the Love of your Brother is yours to absorb;
the Teaching of That One is yours to hear.
Know this, My friends, and take responsibility for reaching your brothers with these truths.

My plan is that the world should be changed by man.
The Law forbids all else.
Therefore, My friends, I depend on you to execute My Plan, and thus prepare the New World.

My Teaching will show you that the Law of God holds for all men.
Naught can stand outside this Law.
When men see this they will gladly accept the simple Law of Love, and make it manifest.

Wherever I look today around the world, I see the shining points of Light of My people, those on whom I rely. These beacons of Light shall bring all men to Me, and thus the Plan will unfold.

May it be that you will gather yourselves around Me in this way, that My Light may kindle your flame; and so together we can transform this world.

The path is not easy, My friends; much there is to do. But through simple Love and Brotherhood, all shall be achieved.

Make no mistake, My friends: Maitreya needs you — needs you to further the Plan which He brings, which is the Plan of God.
I trust you, My friends, not to forsake Me.

May the Divine Light and Love and Power of the One Most Holy God be now gathered around you all.

Message No. 86

October 17, 1979

My dear friends, I am happy indeed to be among you once again.

My friends, My dear ones, My comrades of old, many times before have I exhorted you to work to prepare My way.
Once again may I say how vital this work is.
The more who know that I have returned, the sooner My face shall be known.
Let My Message speak to all men.
Let My words go forth.
Send them to your brothers near and far and awaken them, too, to My Advent.

My public work proceeds.
I plan from day to day and watch carefully man's response.
In this way the rhythm of My Emergence is set, and so you see, My friends, how your work influences My Plan.

My Masters will show you that there is little which you cannot effect if you but try.
All is possible to man.
All that man needs is provided by his Source.
The Great Provider remembers His children.
Look not then askance at the future time but welcome it with open arms and joy, knowing that Brotherhood and Trust will be the norm.

My friends, My brothers and sisters, take stock of where
you now stand.
Are you ready to go with Me to the Blessed Isle of Love?
Are you ready to share with all that which you now have?
Are you prepared, My friends, to look Life bravely in the
eye and see it as a challenge of achievement?
Naught can hold you back if you go with Me.
Nothing will remain of the old inertia, but clasped in
Light and Love, you, My friends, can know the joy of
nearness to the Father, that joy which it is My privilege to
bestow on you.
Take then, My friends, your courage in your hands and
follow Me back to your Source.
Naught can go wrong, My friends: Maitreya is with you!

May the Divine Light and Love and Power of the
Everlasting God be now manifest within your hearts and
minds.
May this manifestation bring you to the achievement of
your own soul's purpose.

Message No. 87

November 16, 1979

My dear friends, I am happy to be among you once more
in this fashion.

My Mission proceeds well, even beyond My expectations.
For this reason alone you may see Me soon.
My plan is to emerge as quickly as may be, and to evoke
from you that Service which, My friends, I know burns
within your hearts.

For many reasons am I here.
Many are the claims upon My Love, My Will, but, above
all, to show you once again that man's purpose is to serve
both God and man am I here.
When you see this, you will enter a field of endeavour
which awaits all those who would go with Me.
Trust Me, My friends; trust that as your Elder Brother I
know the way, for that Way, My friends, has been
trodden by all Those Whom you call Master.
The Way to God, My brothers, is through Service and
Love.
That simple Path shall I place before you and invite you
to tread.

My dear friends, look around you at the happenings in the
world and ask yourselves:
"Is this not strange? How come we by this new
light?"
If you are true to the Light within you, you will see that
My Presence evokes this change.
Thus will you know that I am here.

Thus can you share the burden of preparation for My
Emergence and thus can you know the joy of Service.
Take upon yourselves, My brothers, a part of this burden;
make it your own; dedicate yourselves to making My
Presence known to your brothers far and near.
In this way can you serve Me and them.

My Teachings go forth.
Many are those now, in My centre, who listen and act,
filled with joy that a new Light is here, a new Promise
beckons, a New World is in the making.
Share soon then, My friends, in this aspiration and truth,
and release the God Who within you dwells.

Take to your hearts, My friends, this message of Hope;
spread it abroad among your brothers and tell them that
Maitreya has come, that the Lord of Love is here.
Tell them this, My friends, and know the bliss of serving
the Truth.

May the Divine Light and Love and Power of the One
Most Holy God enter now your hearts and minds and
bring you to the realisation of your divinity.

Message No. 88

November 20, 1979

My friends, I am happy indeed to be among you once more in this way.

I come to tell you that My Plan proceeds smoothly and well.
All proceeds to plan; all My hopes are being fulfilled, and the Day of Declaration draws near.

Soon will you see Me in full vision and, as you do, realise that for many this meeting is not the first.
Many of you have served Me before, long, long ago, and, coming now into the world, stand ready once again.
Know this, My friends, and seize the opportunity now offered to serve Me and the world.
Know this, My brothers, and take part in this Plan of God for your fulfilment.
Many are the ways to serve; many are the paths of ascent.
No-one today need feel deprived of a mode of service, of a path forward to the future.
All paths, all means, flow to God.
Take, My friends, the nearest of these paths and with Me serve your brothers.

When you see Me, you will see a Friend, a Helper, not a God.
Know this, My brothers, and work with Me as equals.
Let fear not cloud the bond between us, but let us together, as friends and brothers, serve the Plan.

The means are simple, as you know.
The way forward is steep but climbable.
The Path of Ascent is signposted.
My Masters will guide you on each turn of that Path, and
show you the next step.

Hold out your hands to Me, My friends, and let Me lift
you into the Light.
Raise your heads to that Light, My brothers, and let Me
show you the face of God.
Kneel with Me before His divine feet and know the joy of
communion with Truth.

Let Me show you, My friends, that you are sons of God.
Let Me take you, My brothers, on the Way to God.
Let Me show you, My dear ones, the image and wonders
of God.

Come with Me and know the New Truth.

May the Divine Light and Love and Power of the One
Most Holy God be now manifest within your hearts and
minds.
May this manifestation bring you to His blessed feet.

Message No. 89

November 28, 1979

My dear friends, I am happy to be with you once again in
this fashion.

My brothers, you have heard something of My Plans, of
My Teachings, and know to look soon for My face.
Thus it is, My friends.
Thus do I speak to your brothers.
Thus do I make known the needs of the time.
Thus will be established in men correct relationship to
man and God.
My Mission is to unfold for you the Divine Plan, to
administer the Will and Purpose of God, and to return
you to your Source.

My Masters, too, stand ready to serve.
Their Ranks will be filled by you, men and women of the
world, and so release Them for the Higher Way.

At the foot of the mountain, My brothers, the climb
upward seems steep indeed; but when the first steps have
been taken, the progress is rapid; and near the mountain
top, winged feet shall you have; and from that height
shall you see the glories of God.
Thus shall it be, My friends and brothers.
I, Maitreya, promise.

Take Me to your hearts as I have taken you to mine.
Work with Me, My friends, and know Me as a Guide.
Help Me to reinstate in the world the Plan of God, the
destined Will of our Divine Source.
Help Me to do this, My friends, and inherit your greatness.

My steps resound.
My Law unfolds.
My words find response in the hearts of many.
The time is not far off when the New World will be seen,
the Country of Love approached,
the City of Truth built.
Take My hands, My friends, and let us together build.

May the Divine Light and Love and Power of the One
Most Holy God be now manifest within your hearts and
minds.
May this manifestation lead you to respond to My
Presence among you.

Message No. 90

December 6, 1979

My dear friends, I am happy indeed to be so close to you once again, and to release to you some further fragments of My Plan.

My work proceeds.
My Law finds response in the hearts of men.
My Love permeates these hearts and awakens in them a new Light.
Thus do I bring to men the knowledge of My Presence.
Thus do I establish in their midst a reservoir of Truth.
Thus do I bring men to the readiness for a Divine Gift.

My purpose tonight is to tell you that My face is seen and known by so many of your brothers that now My Message bears fruit.
They respond to Me as you, My friends, will do when you see Me; when My Love surrounds you as it now surrounds them; as My simple Truth raises the Light in you, and you embrace that Truth.

I am the Messenger of God's Truth.
I am the Perfect One.
I am the Means to the Light.
I make smooth the Path for all men.
I condition God's Truth.
I wield the Sword.
I embody God's Plan.
I am the Exponent of Love.
I am the Manipulator of Will.
I am the Revealer of Truth.

Take That which I am within your hearts and reveal the
God you are.

I shall place before you all the purpose of God.
I shall lead before the Throne of God all who are ready.
I shall kneel with you at His divine feet and together shall
we salute His grace.

I am the Intention of God.
I am the Revealer of God's Law.
I am the Truth embodied.
I am Cause and Knowledge of Cause.
I am Love Itself.
I come before you as a simple Man.
I come as a Brother and Friend.
I shall return you to your Source.
I am among you till the end of the Age.

My Love surrounds you always.
My heart beats in rhythm with yours.
My hand shall guide you and protect you.
My Love has no bounds.
Know Me as your Friend and Counsellor.
See God through Me.

Take That which I am within your hearts and become the
Gods you are.
Take within you That which I give and reveal the Light.
Accept My Gift and know the Source.

May the Divine Light and Love and Power of the One
Most Holy God be now manifest within your hearts and
minds.
May this manifestation lead you to serve in the
accomplishment of My Mission.

Message No. 91

December 12, 1979

My dear friends, I am happy indeed to be with you once
more in this fashion.

My friends, I am emerging so quickly now that little time
will elapse until you see My face.
When you see Me, you will know that your Brother of
Old, Maitreya Himself, is among you.
I shall call on you to work for Me and for the Plan.
I know, My friends, that I may count on you.

My Teaching is this:
learn to share, to grasp your brother's hand and know him
as yourself.
Teach this simple Truth and you teach the Law of God.

My Presence creates an atmosphere of new trust, of new
possibilities for mutual understanding.
Seize, then, these God-given opportunities to grow in
Service.

My Masters are Themselves returning to the world; One
by One, They take up Their stations among you.
Soon Their Presence will more potently be felt, and in
this way shall They establish the New Vanguard, those
whose task it is to build the structures of the coming time.
May you know Them before long.
May you give Them your trust and work with Them for
your brothers.

Know Me as One of yourselves, as a simple man indeed, come among you to serve you and guide you, to teach you and love you, to show you the Path to God.

Many are gathering around Me now.
My Army grows.
My Light embraces all.
My Love fills their hearts.
My Will upholds them.
My Shield covers them.
My Truth inspires them.

You, too, My friends, can find the path to My Ranks.
Take it quickly, My brothers, and advance with Me.

May the Divine Light and Love and Power of the One Most Holy God be now manifest within your hearts and minds.
May this manifestation lead you to find Me quickly, and to serve at My side.

Message No. 92

December 19, 1979

My dear friends and disciples, I am happy indeed to be
with you once again in this fashion.

My need for disciples who realise the dangers of the time
is great.
I need, also, those who sense My Presence to make
known this Promise to their brothers.
All who share the hope that mankind should live in peace
together work for Me.
Peace, Sharing and Justice are central to My Teaching.
Wherever the Light of these Truths shines I turn My eye,
and through the channel of that Light do I send My Love.
Thus do I work.
Thus through you do I change the world.

My friends, I need you in other ways:
I need your capacity for Joy, to awaken this divine aspect
in the hearts of all men, to show them that ahead of
mankind stretches the luminous path of Truth, the direct
Path to the Source.
Manifested Love and Joy will take you quickest there.

My friends, My brothers and sisters, I need you too to act
for Me, to state aloud My intentions, My requirements as
the Representative of God:
to show men that the world is One;
that men are brothers;
that the Law of Love and Justice must be implemented if
mankind would survive.
Tell your brothers this, My friends, and prepare them for
Me.

Awaken in their hearts the readiness to share, and light their lamp.
Create an atmosphere of love and joy and pave smooth My way.
Manifest the Love which I send you, demonstrate the Gods which you are, and usher in a new and better time.
Do this for Me, My friends and brothers, and rejoice soon in My Appearance among you.

My Emergence proceeds.
My Plans unfold.
My message at this time of joyous celebration is this: awaken anew the Love in the hearts of your brothers and teach them to share.

My plan is that you shall see Me soon.
When you do, you will see your Friend and Brother of Old, the Advocate of Love, the Administrator of Will, the Creator through you of the New and Blessed Time.

May the Divine Light and Love and Power of the One Most Holy God be now manifest within your hearts and minds.
May this manifestation lead you to realise your true usefulness to Me and to the Plan.

Message No. 93

January 22, 1980

My dear friends, I am happy indeed to be so close to you once again.

My Mission continues with success.
My heart enfolds all who think of Me.
My Love embraces all who love their brothers.
Know this to be true and call on My aid.

When you see Me, you will know that there is among you now a simple Man of God, a Man like other men, but One Who from time long past has followed a certain Path, Who knows well that Path and can lead you thereon.
That Path to God, My friends, is the Treasure I hold for you.
Awaken your minds and hearts to this possibility, and reach the goal.
The Way is simple, the Way is sure.
My Teaching will guide you there.

No man need fear for the future when My Shield shall cover him.
No man need fear want when My Principle governs.
No man need feel separate from God when My Way beckons.

Hold yourselves in readiness for My words.
Take your places at My side.
Make manifest the God within, and transform the world.

My heart aches when I see so many needlessly die;
hunger and pestilence stalk the Earth.
Nothing so moves Me to grief as this shame.
The crime of separation must be driven from this world.
I affirm that as My Purpose.

I address you tonight as those who seek the truth.
My friends, the Truth stands among you.
The Truth is in your hearts.
The Truth, My friends, My brothers and sisters, is Love
and Sharing, Justice and Freedom.
Make these manifest in your lives and communities, and
re-establish the Plan of God.

My voice will soon be heard, My Teaching known, My
Love felt.
May it be that you will quickly see Me, come towards
Me, gather around Me, work with Me, know Me and love
Me, know God and love God through Me.

May the Divine Light and Love and Power of the One
Most Holy God be now manifest within your hearts and
minds.
May this manifestation reveal to you your true worth as
children of God.

Message No. 94

January 31, 1980

My dear friends, once again I am with you and am happy
to be so.

My plans unfold.
My Mission prospers.
My way is being cleared.
Many now in the world know of My Presence and help in
all ways.
Still more is needed from you who believe, My friends.
If in a final major effort you can inform the world that I
am here, My face will shortly be seen by all.
I trust you, My brothers and sisters, to work thus for Me.

When you see Me, you will understand the reasons for
your presence in the world.
You are here, My friends, to serve the Plan of God.
You are here, each of you, from love of your brothers.
You are here, too, to learn, to expand your knowledge of
that Plan and to progress along the Path.
That is the truth of your existence at this time.
Take heed, then, of this opportunity which I present to
you: to share with Me in My work of succour, to ease My
burden, to unfold the God within you and to lead your
brothers to the Light.

Many there are whom I call.
Many there are who wait and listen.
Few there are, indeed, who seize the time and act.
These few are My people.
May you become one of them.

Let Me say this, My friends:
without your willing help, naught may be done.
I come to lead and teach, not to enforce.
Take, then, to your hearts this, My Appeal, and work with
Me, for Me, for your brothers, and so save the world.

Many hear Me now and give Me their trust, attune their
thoughts to Me and follow My lead.
Soon will emerge a body of prepared men who know the
needs of the time, who live to serve, who love their
brothers.
Make yourselves one with them and follow Me. I shall
lead you not astray.

May the Divine Light and Love and Power of the One
Most Holy God be now manifest within your hearts and
minds.
May this manifestation lead you in Light to the feet of
God.

Message No. 95

February 14, 1980

My dear friends, I am happy to be among you once more in this way, and to tell you that My first phase of Emergence is almost complete.

Within weeks, many more of your brothers shall see Me.
Within months, a large section of the world will know that I am here.
Whether they recognise Me or not, My face will be seen.

I tell you this, My friends:
look hard and listen well, for My voice is being heard,
My words are turning the hearts of men to the Truth.
My Love pervades the hearts of all those who seek that Truth, who long for its establishment and thus prepare My way.

First of all, you will see a simple Man, One of yourselves.
Know Him as a Man Who has traveled for long on the Path to God, Who seeks to take you with Him on that Sacred Way and lead you to His divine feet.

Take My simple words to your hearts.
There let them blossom and flower and bring forth the Light.
Take, too, to your hearts My Love.
Send this to your brothers and make light the dark.
Hold fast to My Purpose, which is to take man to God.
Help Me thus, My friends, and serve well the Plan.

My Teachings are simple, My words likewise.
All that I say is quickly understood.
There is nothing difficult about the Truth of God.
The Truth of God, My friends, resides in the hearts of all
men.
That simplicity is yours to unfold.
I, your Guide, shall show you the way.

The time has come to show My face on a wider scale.
In this way, men will know that the Son of Man is among
them once more.

The Love of God manifests through Me; the bliss of that
Love is yours to take.
Stretch forth your hands, My friends and brothers, and
sup well, drink deeply of the Blessing of God.

May the Divine Light and Love and Power of the One
Most Holy God be now manifest within your hearts and
minds.
May this manifestation lead you to see quickly the Light,
the Love and the Truth which I bring.

Message No. 96

February 19, 1980

My dear friends, My dear ones, I am happy indeed to be among you once more in this fashion.

My Task begins.
As I emerge, I shall place before the world the necessity for change.
These changes, My friends, are God-given.
Man requires, as he moves towards God, to demonstrate that divinity.
All man's structures must shine with the Divine Light.
All man's ways of thought must reveal the God within.
This truth, My friends, is at the basis of change.
When you see this, you will gladly accept this need.

My friends, I am with you tonight in a special way, in a new form, closer than ever before, to awaken in you the light of the Truth which I bring.
That Truth, My friends, is Brotherhood and Sharing, Justice and Love.
Where these aspects are present, you will know Me.

Take heart from all I say, My brothers, for the way ahead for man shines brightly indeed.
Naught there is to fear, My friends, for all will be well.
My Mission prospers, and My Presence guarantees this future.

I am here tonight to tell you that soon for yourselves you shall see and hear Me.
Make this time shorter, if you will, and make known My Presence.

When you see Me, you will see your Friend and Brother,
One Who for long has waited for this time, to clasp again
the hands of His brothers and to share their life.

My friends, My Presence is established, My Love flows
to you, My Joy will be yours, My Truth shared, My
Father known.
With your help, all will be achieved.

My task is to show you the Way to God, to outline that
simple Path, to take your hand and lead you to His divine
feet, and so complete His Plan.
My Masters are with you also.
In gathering numbers They shall be among you.
When you see Us, you will know that
the time of God has come,
the Age of Reason and Love begun,
the meaning of Life restored,
the principle of Love demonstrated,
the Will of God fulfilled.

May the Divine Light and Love and Power of the One
Most Holy God be now manifest within your hearts and
minds.
May this manifestation lead you in trust to My side.

Message No. 97

February 28, 1980

My beloved friends, I am happy indeed to be so close to you once again.

My Plan is to reveal My Presence shortly on a much wider scale and to show men that the New Age is dawning, that the recipe for change is Sharing and Brotherhood, Justice and Love.
To My Banner I shall call those who would walk with Me.

Join My Army, My friends and brothers, and cleanse this world of hate.
Sharpen the Sword of Love, My brothers, close your ranks around Me, and valiantly together into the future let us march.

My Principles take hold of men's minds.
My Love penetrates their hearts.
My simple words find response, and My Law begins to govern.
Thus may you say with Me, My Friends, that the future for man is bright, that the Love of God is established abroad, and the Law shall flourish.

Many there are who doubt My Presence.
Many there are who seek for Me in vain, looking upwards to the sky and, finding Me not, cast Me out from their hearts.
The simple truth, My brothers, is that I am a Man among men, living among you as such, knowing and feeling your griefs and needs, loving and caring for you, desiring to share with you the Blessings of God.

Look upon Me thus, My friends and brothers, and know the meaning of Trust, know the value of Love, know the blessings of God's Plan for all men.

May you be ready when I appear before you.
May you be ready for the changes which must ensue.
May you gladly, eagerly, accept these changes and make new this world.
Naught stands still on Earth, My friends; all must change and die.
The dead remnants of the past must likewise find themselves as ashes.
From these ashes shall arise the Temple of God, the City of Love.
May you know this to be true.
I am with you always.

May the Divine Light and Love and Power of the One Most Holy God be now manifest within your hearts and minds.
May this manifestation lead you to be ever mindful of your true nature as Gods.

Message No. 98

March 5, 1980

My dear friends and disciples, I am with you once more.

My heart embraces you all.
My Love enfolds you.
My Law will guide you.
My Teaching will show you the path to the Source.
Hold steadfast to the truth of your Being and follow Me.

My Way is a simple way indeed.
Naught hinders on the Path to God through Love.
This I shall teach.
This shall I demonstrate, and when you see how simple is
this Way, My Plans shall become yours.

My Masters are gathering in strength.
My Forces expand.
My simple means attract the good in man.
When you see Me, you will know that the time has come
to serve, to lift yourselves and your brothers through
service to the world.
This way, My Way, will take you quickly to God.
My Masters, too, know this Path and under Their
instruction shall you realise your Godhead.

My purpose is to show men that he need fear no more,
that all of Light and Truth rests within his heart, that
when this simple fact is known, man will become God.

God's nature is to love.
God's purpose is to serve.
God is known through Sharing and Justice.

Spread abroad these simple Truths, My friends, and
perform a mighty act.

My Presence will soon be known to all.
My face will soon be seen by many.
My words shall touch the hearts of all those who love
their brothers and thus work with Me.
Make it your resolve, My friends, to work thus for the
world and speed the inauguration of the Age of Beauty,
Reason and Love.

May the Divine Light and Love and Power of the One
Most Holy God be now manifest within your hearts and
minds.
May this manifestation take you swiftly to the heart of the
Great Father.

Message No. 99

March 11, 1980

My dear friends, I am happy to be with you once more.

My methods produce results.
From My point of vision, great changes can be seen.
Therefore, My friends, I have decided to emerge into full
and public work more quickly than planned.
So, My friends, you shall the sooner see Me.

May I ask you, My brothers and sisters, to act as My
agents, to tell your friends and those you meet that
Maitreya is here, that the Son of Man walks abroad once
more, that the Teacher for the New Age is among you,
and that that Age has begun.
Speak thus, My friends and brothers, and know the joy of
Service.
Speak thus, My dear ones, and light a lamp for Me.

When you see Me, you will know that you have not
worked in vain, that your Brother of Old is with you,
that your Friend and Guide is among you,
that your Teacher of Old has returned to show you the
simple Path to God.
Wherefore, then, My friends, your fear?
Make it your task to do this for Me, and take within your
hands the reins of progress.

My Plans are laid.
My Masters silently enter Their centres.
One by One, They take Their places among you.
My joy is unbounded as I watch the response of mankind.

My simple Truth, that God and Love are One, is
awakening man to the promise of the future.
This makes simple My Task.
My friends, show yourselves as men and women ready to
act as heroes, as warriors of old, filled with Joy and Love,
ready for the tasks of succour and love which will fall to
you.
Have no fear, My brothers: your shoulders shall be
strengthened by Me.

Take care to miss Me not.
Watch and listen.
My face appears.
My voice is being heard.
Know Me as your Master and Friend, Teacher and
Brother, Guide and Messenger of God.

May the Divine Light and Love and Power of the One
Most Holy God be now manifest within your hearts and
minds.
May this manifestation lead you to see yourselves and
each other as the Gods you are.

Message No. 100

My dear friends, I am happy to be with you at this centenary, as you might call it.

My friends, I am near you indeed.
I see around you your aspiration and love, your hope and desire for a better world.
Believe Me, My friends, all these will be fulfilled.
That New World is now in the making, is formed in thought and desire, and slowly descends.
Therefore, My brothers, know no fear.
I am among you in many ways.
I present Myself to the world in many facets.
I galvanise all forms to change.
I stimulate all souls to growth.
I am with you and in you.
I am the Heart of your life.
I seek to place before you the Laws which are God.
I aim to evoke from you the love of your heart.

I am the Prince of Peace.
I am the Sword Bearer.
I am in your hearts as Love.
I am your Friend and Guide.
I am the Lawgiver.
I know God's Purpose.
I teach His Plan.
I long to serve.
I greet the New Day.
I bring Joy.
I awaken the New Spirit in man.
I come prepared for My Ttask.

I call you as helpers.
I take you by the hand to the Source.
I shall live among you.

My Teaching goes forth.
The New Day beckons.
The Real takes root.
The Time of God has come.
My Way beckons all men.
My Travail will not be in vain.
My Justice shall be done.
My Army shall triumph.

By pure Love man will achieve.
By great deeds man will conquer.
By mighty steps man will advance into the future.
By My help all shall be achieved.

My name is Oneness.
My Love abideth.
My Law creates.
My Teaching shall turn all men to God.

My Masters stand ready.
The Day is at hand.
The Prophecies of Old are being fulfilled.
The Dark Ones tremble.
The Law shall be upheld.
The Name of God is Love.
I am His Messenger.

May the Divine Light and Love and Power of the One
Most Holy God be now manifest within your hearts and
minds.
May this manifestation lead you quickly to see yourselves
as units of God.

Message No. 101

March 26, 1980

My dear friends, I am happy indeed to be with you once more in this fashion.

Before long, My friends, you shall see Me.
You shall witness in fact the Return of your Brother of Old.
You shall see thus the fulfilment of the Plan of God, for the Fiat of God has brought Me here.
Likewise, mankind itself has called Me, and gladly have I answered that call.

Justice must and shall be done.
The world groans for Justice.
The true reason for man's problems today is the absence of Justice and Love.
Were these divine aspects to be in force tomorrow, a new sweetness would colour your lives.
This gracious gift of Love and Just Sharing stems from God.
Only through its correct manifestation can God be known.
Teach men this, My friends, and you teach a great and simple Truth.

When men see Me, My brothers, they will see a simple and just Man.
All who know God manifest these qualities.
Seek, then, for Me in that guise.

Now that My Presence is an established fact, I can see more clearly the problems of man.

These are manifold, My friends, but stem from a simple
cause.

Simple lack of Love is the root of man's suffering today.
Naught but this holds him from the manifestation of his
divine potential.
All of Godhead exists in man, but without Love naught
but suffering ensues.
For long, My friends, have you known this; many times
before have you heard the need for Love.
Nevertheless, that divine aspect is wanting in your lives.

I come to show you the simple Path to God through Love,
to teach you the techniques of Love, the way forward
through Love and Justice, correct relationship of man to
man and thus to God.

Know then this simple Man when you see Him and call
Him Brother, for it is as a Brother of all men that I appear:
to take you by the hand and lead you to the Father,
to show you the wondrous vision of your future,
to establish in you the will to serve,
to create with you the City of Truth,
the Temple of Love,
to lead you forwards, and back to God.

May the Divine Light and Love and Power of the One
Most Holy God be now manifest within your hearts and
minds.
May this manifestation take you with Me back to your
Source.

Message No. 102

April 3, 1980

My dear friends, I am happy indeed to be among you once again in this fashion, and to release to you a fragment of My Teaching and Plan.

We are together, you and I, for the same purpose.
You, My friends, are here because in your hearts you love all men, feel responsible for the world, respond to human need and long to serve.
That, likewise, is My Purpose today.
I, too, feel the needs of man, the need of all men everywhere to live and work with dignity and trust.
The need to serve conditions My existence.
The Love of My heart draws Me to you.
We are together therefore, you and I, to serve.
Knowing this, grasp the opportunity to serve the world in a unique fashion, My friends, and travel far on the Path.
Why sit and wait for My Appearance when the world needs your weight?
I ask you then to work with Me, to prepare My way before men, and to induce, somewhat, the climate of hope in which, readily, My face may be seen.

Count yourselves as fortunate, My brothers, to be presented with such a choice.
The day is coming when you will thank your Maker for this opportunity.

My plans proceed steadily and well.
My face and words become known. Many now respond to My Teaching and take up My Cause.

Soon a new wave of interest in the Truth will be evoked from man, and on that wave My face shall be seen.

Count yourselves as My friends, and work with Me. Know yourselves as My partners, and help the world. Reveal yourselves as My disciples, and create the New World.

Perhaps you are impatient to see My face — this is natural.
Shortly, My friends, you shall see the face of your Brother of Old, your Teacher of long past, your Friend and Guide, your Master and Servant, your Elder Brother. You shall see the face of a simple Man indeed. And from among your brothers you shall pick Me out and, saluting the God in Me, shall know Me for what I am. And together in Love shall we make all things new.
Maitreya has said it.

May the Divine Light and Love and Power of the Everlasting God be now manifest within your hearts and minds.
May this manifestation lead you to see and to know the truth of your own Being.

Message No. 103

April 10, 1980

My dear friends, it is with pleasure that I speak to you
again in this way.

My Truth is beginning to condition men's lives.
Despite appearances all proceeds to plan, and I, Maitreya,
am not disheartened.
Many are the changes, subtle and gross, which are being
forged by My Presence.
Much that is harmful to man is being destroyed.
Much of good blossoms in its stead.
Know this to be so and fear not.

When you see Me, you will know that I have come to
teach you a knowledge which in part you know.
All men everywhere have heard the truth of Brotherhood.
They know that Love and Justice are basic to life.
Nevertheless, My friends, naught but chaos reigns, and
Justice is hard to find.

My Presence will evoke from men the capacity for Joy,
for Just Sharing and Love.
For this am I here.
Know this to be so and fear not.

My Presence evokes in man a new sense of wonder.
Looking within and around him, man senses vistas of
knowledge of which he cannot dream; of Wisdom to
which he can but aspire; the expression of Love which he
knows to be his own.
Know this to be so and have no fear.

My aim is to teach you the truth of God and of
yourselves;
to outline for you a path to the future which is the Way to
God;
to create with you the shining Temple of Truth;
to live among you in the City of Love;
to work with you for the Plan of God.

My Emergence proceeds.
Soon your brothers in My centre will know that among
them now is a simple Man of God, a Brother among
brothers, a Spokesman for them: to place before the
nations the needs of all men for a world at peace, for Just
Sharing of resources, for laughter and Joy, for the creation
of a New World built on the Pattern of God.

May the Divine Light and Love and Power of the One
Most Holy God be now manifest within your hearts and
minds.
May this manifestation lead you to see and to know My
Presence in your midst.

Message No. 104

April 15, 1980

My dear friends, I am happy indeed to be with you once again in this fashion and to tell you that all is well. All proceeds to plan, and that Plan works out.

When My face is seen on a wider scale, you will know that your Elder Brother is with you, a Brother Who comes to teach you the Ways of God, Who loves you and desires to serve you.

From your ranks I shall choose My helpers.
May it be that you shall find yourselves among them.
My need is for those who love both God and man, who see each in themselves and who long to serve the Plan.
Whether that Plan is known to you or not, you can serve your brothers.
All that is needed is the love of God in your hearts.
All that is required is the blessing of Trust and desire for Justice.
Where these aspects are present, I shall recognise My warriors.

Prepare to see Me very soon.
Prepare to recognise Me, to trust Me, to love Me and work with Me, for I come to teach you the way to the Source of your Being, to your very core.
When you know Me, you will find that I have ever been within your heart.
My Call has been heard by you for long, and you are here in answer to that Call.
Knowing this, take up the challenge which I present and help Me to serve your brothers.

Take care to miss Me not.
Watch carefully, My friends, and be happy at the prospect.
Smilingly turn your gaze on the future.
Laughingly turn your back on the past.
Gratefully receive the blessing of God's Love and create anew the Plan.
Make haste to follow.
Make haste to recognise.
Triumphantly teach and know the joy of Service.
My Love goes with you all.

May the Divine Light and Love and Power of the One Most Holy God be now manifest within your hearts and minds.
May this manifestation lead you in gladness to your Brother's side.

Message No. 105

June 5, 1980

My dear friends and disciples, I am indeed glad to have this further opportunity to speak to you in this fashion.

My purpose tonight is to tell you that all proceeds well, even ahead of plan.
This being so, My next public appearance will take place a few short weeks from now, and in a fashion broader than before.
Hitherto, My Appearance has been restricted to a certain section.
From now, My plan is to reach a wider sphere.
In this way, under Law, My Emergence takes place.

Within your hands, My friends, rests the key to this Appearance.
Make known the fact of My Presence among you and speed My Emergence.
Far and wide make known this truth and gather to Me your brothers and sisters.

When you see and hear Me, you will realise that you have known for long the Truths which I utter.
Within your hearts rests the Truth of God.
These simple truths, My friends, underlie all existence.

Sharing and Justice, Brotherhood and Freedom are not new concepts.
From the dawn of time mankind has linked his aspiration to these beckoning stars.
Now, My friends, shall we anchor them in the world.

Through you, My friends, if you will, I may work.
Through you, My dear friends, I shall change the world.
Through your willing service, My dear ones, the New
Age shall be built.
Take upon yourselves this challenge.
Take upon your shoulders this burden of Light.
Help Me, My friends and brothers, to establish that Light
in the world and create for all men the circumstance of
Peace and Joy.

My Appearance to you is near.
Look closely, My friends, and miss Me not.
Take Me to your hearts and make Me your Friend.
Accept Me as yours and follow Me to your Source.

May the Divine Light and Love and Power of the One
Most Holy God be now manifest within your hearts and
minds.
May this manifestation lead you in gladness to His
shining feet.

Message No. 106

My dear friends, I am happy indeed to be with you once again in this way.

Happy I am, too, to see around your heads the light of Aspiration and Love.
These aspects, My friends, will bring you safely to the feet of God.

Let Me speak to you once more about Love, about Sharing and Justice, for these are the basis and the crown of your lives.
When mankind knows Love, Justice and Sharing, mankind will know God.

May it not be that you have heard of Love before, yet find it difficult to manifest?
Why should this be so, My friends, when your nature is Love Itself?
Essentially you are God, and God and Love are One.
Manifest That which you are, My brothers and sisters, and become the Gods that you are.
There is no quicker way to God than through the manifestation of Love, Justice and Service.
Serve and grow in Love, My friends, and realise your Godhead.

Grow through Love and Service, and come with Me to your Source.
Let Me lead you thereto, My brothers, and let us stand together before the Shining One, kneel at His divine feet and know the bliss of the Peace of God.

When you see Me, you will see a simple Brother and
Friend, but One Who knows the Path to God, has trodden
it long before and seeks to teach you the Way.
Let Me show you, My friends, that this simple Way is
open to all men.
I shall help you place your feet on that Luminous Path
and shall guide you to Him.

Make haste to know Me.
Make haste to serve Me.
Make known My Presence among you.
Be ready to listen.
Judge wisely.
Grasp your brother's hand, and together in trust shall we
change the world.

May the Divine Light and Love and Power of the One
Most Holy God be now manifest within your hearts and
minds.
May this manifestation take you quickly and lightly to the
feet of God.

Message No. 107

July 3, 1980

My dear friends, I am happy indeed to be with you once more in this way, and to tell you that My Emergence proceeds apace.

Shortly, now, many more of your brothers shall become aware of My Presence.
I shall speak to them of Love, of the need for the manifestation of this divine principle, so that all men may live within the Aura of God.
God and Love are identical.
When man loves, he takes a step to God.
This Path of Love, My simple Way, will take man surely to his Source.

The major need today is for the transformation of the structures within which you now live.
Your civilisation, My friends, is dying — nay, it is already dead.
Out of its ashes will grow a new beauty, whose basis is Love, Justice and Sharing.
Make these your aims, My friends, and know the meaning of God.
Make these your aims, My friends, and know the meaning of a full and happy life.
Consecrate yourselves to these divine aspects, My brothers, and fulfil the Plan.

My Teaching is simple.
I speak in simple terms.
All men may understand Me.
All men can love Me.

You will know this to be true when you see My face, for that face, My friends, sits ever within the hearts of those who love their brothers.

My Masters likewise are returning among you.

Taking up Their posts within your cities, They are teaching the ways of the New Time, establishing within your ranks your leaders, those who know the Plan.

May you quickly see and recognise Them and give Them your support.

All goes well, My friends; there is no need to fear.

The cloud of despair is lifting from the Earth.

My Presence vouchsafes this to you.

Make known My Presence among you, and speed My Emergence.

Make known My Presence among you, and lift the hearts of your brothers.

Make known My Presence, and be assured of My constant Love.

My heart opens towards you.

My Will sustains you.

My Law shall guide you.

My Teaching shall bring you to God.

Take within you That which I give, and show it to the world.

Release within you That which you are, and show the Spirit of Love.

Take My hand, My friends, and let us together walk into the radiant future.

My Blessing goes with you all.

May the Divine Light and Love and Power of the One Most Holy God be now manifest within your hearts and minds.

May this manifestation lead you to see Me quickly; and seeing, know Me; and knowing, serve Me.

Message No. 108

September 4, 1980

My dear friends, I am happy indeed to be among you once more in this fashion.

Much has happened in the world since I spoke last to you. Much of good has taken place, much that concerns the future of all men and all things in the world.
In the first place, My Message prospers. My team of workers grows, and steadily the voice of Truth is heard.
When you see Me, you will know that My voice is yours, for I speak for all men and women everywhere.
I speak the thoughts which blossom in hearts and minds of pure Love.
I speak of the needs of all, for Sharing and Justice.
I show men that the path to Justice is simple, the way forward calls all men.
I speak of God's Truth, of the Light within mankind, of the need for Trust, the Love of brother for brother.
Of all of this I speak.

Soon men will know that their Representative is among them, their Guide and Leader.
Trusting shall they respond, and I shall show the way into the New and Blessed Time.

Many are the forces ranged against us, against the Truth of God; but, My friends, victory is assured.
Have no doubt of this.
My Plan is God's Plan.
Naught can withstand His Will.

Soon you will see that the way forward is simpler than you thought.
The way forward, My friends, has called you from the beginning.
The way to the future and the way to God are united in My Plan.
As you place your foot on the path to Justice and Love, so do you begin the ascent to God.
Nothing, essentially, changes with God.

My friends, My hope is high; likewise should be yours.
Make manifest that hope and glad enterprise, and prepare the path for me.
Make known that I am here.
Make known the fact of My Return.

Call your brothers to Me and joyously spread these glad tidings.
Naught that you could do would furnish better for you your future.
My Blessings go with you all.

May the Divine Light, Love and Will of the Everlasting God be now manifest within your hearts and minds.
May this manifestation lead you quickly to work for My Cause.

Message No. 109

September 11, 1980

I am with you once more, My dear friends and co-workers.

My heart leaps with joy to see the light of Aspiration shining brightly around you.
This confirms for Me My estimation of workers in the Light.
Many there are today who stand ready to serve, awaiting only the Call from Me.
That Clarion Call shall resound throughout the world and draw men of Truth to My side.
Wherefore, then, is the need to fear?
All shall be made well in this coming time.
I, Maitreya, declare this to be so.
I, Maitreya, pledge My word: all shall be well. All manner of things shall be well.
Therefore, My friends, fear not.
Uphold the Light in men's hearts, the hope and trust in the future, and bring them to Me.

My plans proceed regularly and well.
Great is the progress being achieved.
Little as yet may appear to you to be done, but, My friends, much of true worth has already been accomplished.
When you see Me you will recognise this, for I shall point to all manner of achievements and endorse this progress.

Why wait for the sight of Me to act, when from yourselves in trust you can perform much?

Take a little in trust, My friends, and act today as the warriors of old, waiting not for confirmation but glad to be in the vanguard.
Make known to all the fact of My Presence and come gladly to My side.
Make known the need for Sharing and Justice and strike a note for Freedom.
Make known, My friends and brothers, that you stand by your brother's side.
Take your brother's hand and lead him to Me.

My Masters are returning One by One.
Soon twelve of My Brothers will be among you.
Through Them and with Them I work.
Let Them lead and guide you into your future glory.

My plan is to show Myself more openly soon.
At each approach to the public My audiences respond more vividly, and thus is prepared My way.

Hold yourselves in readiness for My face, My words, My simple Teaching, and respond from your hearts.

May the Divine Light and Love and Power of the One Most Holy God be now manifest within your hearts and minds.
May this manifestation lead you to take part in this great manifestation of God's Will.

Message No. 110

September 24, 1980

My dear friends, I am happy indeed to be with you once more in this fashion.

My plan proceeds.
My intentions work out.
My Love registers itself in the hearts of men, and all soon shall feel My Presence.
Wherever you look today, you see the results of change.
Much is happening which causes fear, but, My friends, naught need be feared while I am among you, for I embody the Will of God.
His Plan for change necessitates destruction of old forms.
This, My friends, is inevitable and will usher in a new beauty.

I came before as a Man unheeded.
I am with you again today to re-establish My Love in your hearts.
When you see Me you will know this and gladly gather round Me.

I am the heart's Love of man.
I am the Peace of God.
I am the Initiator of the Little Ones.
I am the Truth enthroned.
I am Light Itself.

I am Love without bounds.
I am close to you.
I am wherever Love manifests.

I am the Creator of a pool of Love from which all men may drink.

Take Me within you and show Me as I am.
Make Me your own and take your brother's hand.
Lead him to Me and serve the Plan.
Love Me and work with Me and know the joy of Service.
Come with Me, My friends, into the New Time, the New World, the New Country of Love.
There let us together adorn ourselves with the Light of Truth, the radiance of God's Love, and kneel before His blessed feet.
My Blessings go with you all.

May the Divine Light and Love and Power of the One Most Holy God be now manifest within your hearts and minds.
May this manifestation bring you quickly to see Me as your Friend and Guide.

Message No. 111

October 6, 1980

My dear friends, I am happy indeed to be among you once more in this fashion.

Great is the progress which is now being made.
Many are those who are turning to the Light of Truth.
Steadily this Light grows, and men await My Presence with expectant desire.

Nothing now stands in the way of My Emergence.
This proceeds in proper rhythm and brings My face before men.
When you yourselves see Me, you will see a Friend and Brother Who has loved you down the ages, has shown you the way before, and comes now to lead you home.

My friends, fear not to act on My behalf.
Trust that I am here and tell your brothers this news.
Make known the need for Justice, for the manifestation of God's Law, and see the commencement of a New and Shining Time.

My friends, there are many who deny My Presence yet act for Me.
Fear not, therefore, for the outcome of My Mission.
All shall be achieved, all hopes fulfilled, and the Promise which I give will be kept.
I shall take you, when you are ready, before the Shining One, and seeing Him shall you know God.

My need for helpers is great.
Help Me then and serve your brothers.
Close your ranks about Me and say nay to the tide of fear.
My Masters will help you through this difficult time and
lead you from the abyss.

My Teaching goes forth.
Simple it is, but remember, My friends, it embodies the
Plan of God.
Where the Plan takes root, no weeds shall grow.
My Blessings go with you all.

May the Divine Light and Love and Power of the One
Most Holy God be now manifest within your hearts and
minds.
May this manifestation lead you swiftly as an arrow to the
heart of God.

Message No. 112

October 14, 1980

My dear friends, I am happy indeed to be with you once more in this way.

My Emergence proceeds as planned.
More than ever now your brothers respond.
When you see Me, you too shall take My Truths to your hearts.
Of this I have no doubt, for I know My people.

Many are those who see a future black indeed.
Wretched in fear, they await the end.
My Promise is this: for all men dawns a future bathed in the light of God's Truth.
Hearken to that truth, My friends, and prove this to be so.

My name shall soon be known, but for the present you will see Me as a Brother among brothers, One of yourselves.
When the Day of Declaration dawns, you will know that that Brother has taught you more than once, has shown you the way to God and released the Teachings of God's Truth.
My friends, the time has come to enlarge that Truth, to show you that to know God is a creative act, to know God is to enter into Deity Itself.
Only thus can we know the truth of our existence.
In this coming time, that knowledge will be yours.

My heart aches for those who needlessly suffer now, when so little change could remedy their lot.

My friends, how can you stand aside and watch while
your brothers die in squalor, in misery and degradation?
My plan is to save these, My children, and show them to
you as brothers.

My plans involve you all.
All who are ready to go with Me into the New Time are
called.
Help Me, My friends, to reconstruct your world, and send
it on its mission of Light.

The time is short indeed when you will see Me.
Make best use of this little time to tell your brothers of
My Presence.
There is naught that you could do more valuable than this.
Hope rises, My friends.
Hope is in your midst.
A new Light dawns in the world, and mankind shall know
Joy.

May the Divine Light and Love and Power of the One
Most Holy God be now manifest within your hearts and
minds.
May this manifestation lead you to see the future in terms
of Joy.

Message No. 113

November 26, 1980

My dear friends, I am happy indeed to be with you once more in this way, and to greet you as a Brother.
That is My true status in relation to mankind, and as a Brother indeed shall I work for you, showing you the simple path to the future, the Lighted Way to God, releasing to you the Laws of God.

My plans proceed well.
All aspects move forward apace.
This being so, little time indeed remains for you to create the climate of hope.
Once again, My friends, I exhort you to this end.
Much may you do by simple means.
Reveal the fact of My Presence in the world and open to the future the hearts of men.

My plans have many phases.
From now I enter one such.
Before this year is out, I shall have completed the phase of approach.
With the dawn of 1981 will begin that of broader sight.
In this immediate coming time, My face will become known to millions.
From that time forth will spread abroad the knowledge of My Presence.
Take then, My friends, your stance in the vanguard and work for Me.

Very many now await My Presence, expect My Return.
How could I disappoint these blessed ones?

No, My friends, from the heart of man has risen the cry
and to that cry for succour have I responded.
Likewise, from Me shall come a cry for help.
From Me shall issue the cry of man's heart.
In your response to that cry of anguish shall you find
your divinity.
Thus shall it be, My friends.
Thus shall I know My people.
Take it upon yourselves to make known My Presence,
and reveal yourselves as Gods.

May the Divine Light and Love and Power of the One
Most Holy God be now manifest within your hearts and
minds.
May this manifestation lead you to see your duty as
workers at My side.

Message No. 114

December 4, 1980

Good evening, My dear friends. I am happy to be with you once more in this fashion.

My Emergence takes place under Law.
All speed is being used, but man himself conditions this progress.
Were you, My friends, to establish a sure climate of hope that I am here, more swiftly indeed would I emerge.
I place before you, therefore, this challenge.
Work thus for Me, My dear friends, and hasten the Plan.

My Masters are taking Their places among you in growing numbers.
Soon a body of twelve such Divine Men will be among you, and will show you with Me the path to the future.
My hands are tied by a Law which binds and limits Me.
You, yourselves, condition My actions.
Make greater use of this responsibility and serve Me and the world.

Prepare to see Me soon.
Prepare to see Me in full physical presence, and miss Me not.
Look for a Man Who will show you the Path to God through Sharing and Justice.
In simple terms indeed shall I speak to you, and bring you to the manifestation of your fullness as Gods.
Hold fast to That which you are, My friends, and allow that God to flourish.

Keep before you the vision of a future bright indeed, and sustain your brothers.
Awaken within them the promise which My Presence brings, and engage their help.

All that I shall do, I shall do through you.
Know this to be true, My friends, and work for Me.
Make known the fact of My Return.
Make known the Promise for all men.
Make known where you stand, My friends, and relieve the lot of your brothers.

Carefully I present My face to the public.
Gradually I become known.
In this way, within the Law, I reveal Myself anew.
Take care, My friends, to miss Me not.
Search well among the teachers.
Grateful am I for the work already done.
My Blessing goes with you all.

May the Divine Light and Love and Power of the One Most Holy God be now manifest within your hearts and minds.
May this manifestation lead you to see each other as yourselves.

Message No. 115

December 9, 1980

I am here, My friends, among you once more, and happy to be so.

My work proceeds well.
My plans enter a new phase.
My horizon widens, and in due time all shall see Me.

My conditions are being met.
Many now in the world accept the need for change, accept that Sharing and Justice are fundamental to man's progress.
This realisation itself will change your world.
Many there are, however, who forget that man is a God, that in all men sits this Divine Being, and who would deny this truth.
Make known, My friends, where you stand in this matter and show your light in the world.
I need all those in whom the Light of Truth shines brightly.
I call on you.
I call you to My side.
Come with Me, My friends, and blaze a path of Light into the future.

My Call does not go unheard.
Many today rejoice at the promise which My Presence brings, but many more by far await still these glad tidings.

Take upon yourselves, My friends, this task:
Make it known that I am here, and embrace My Cause.
Work thus for your brothers and know the joy of Service.
Reveal thus, My friends, the God within.

The timing of My Emergence is precise.
All goes according to this plan.
Look, then, for a Man Who speaks of Sharing and Justice,
a Man like yourselves, of simplicity and Truth.
Take My hand, My friends, and let us walk blithely
together into the radiant future.

Can you not hear the Call? It issues from My heart.
Can you not hear the cry of anguish? It issues from the
heart of man.
That cry has brought Me here.

May the Divine Light and Love and Power of the One
Most Holy God be now manifest within your hearts and
minds.
May this manifestation lead you onward on the Path to
God.

Message No. 116

December 18, 1980

My dear friends, I am happy to greet you at this time of joyous celebration, and to speak to you once again of Love.

Blessed Love, My brothers and sisters, is the nature of God.
This, theoretically, you know perhaps, but how often does it manifest?
With Us, My friends, Love is central to Our lives.
My Brothers and I form the Centre of Love in this world.
I am its Heart, and from the Heart of Love Itself flow Wisdom and Joy.
Know these, My dear friends, and know the nature of God.

My Disciples work to establish in your hearts the capacity for Love.
When that divine aspect becomes manifest within you, My Rod of Power shall bring you within Our Ranks.
Make haste to join Us then, and fulfil your lives.

My brothers, the world longs for Love, for the manifestation of Brotherhood and Justice.
Help Me to create in the world that Blessed Joy.
Take your place at My side, and work as never before.
Help Me, My friends, to create a pool of Love so deep that all men may quench their thirst.

My Teaching is simple: Justice and Love, Sharing and Peace will bring men to God.
Thus has it always been.
Know this and follow Me.

My plans for the future are set.
My Emergence quickens.
My face shall be seen by millions, and soon the world
will take heed.
May this, My friends, sharpen your appetite for My Cause.
Work well, My friends, and present to your brothers the
promise of My Presence.
Much may be learned from a study of your books, but
much more by far from service to the world.
Serve then, My brothers, and play your destined parts.

My Cause shall triumph.
My Law shall flourish.
My Love shall bring together all men.
My Blessings go with you all.
Good night, My dear friends.

May the Divine Light and Love and Power of the One
Most Holy God be now manifest within your hearts and
minds.
May this manifestation itself show you the Path to God.

Message No. 117

February 5, 1981

My dear friends, I am happy indeed to be among you once again in this way.

Many are the changes which result from My Presence among you.
Many are the events which now unfold.
Watch carefully, My friends, and read the signs.

My Hosts expand.
My Army grows in strength.
My warriors stand ready for the fray, and My Generals take horse.
In this way, My brothers and sisters, all is being made ready.

My plan is being fulfilled.
My Love kindles a new aspect in man, and the New Light dawns.
My Promise is this: soon for yourselves you will see a changing world, a world which alters before your eyes.
The old gives way to the new, and man stands on the threshold of Truth.

Where are you going, My friends:
are you with Me or forever against Me and your brother, for My task is to show you that the way for man is the sure Path of Love.

Through Justice and Sharing, that Love, My brothers, will become manifest.
Take heed, then, of My words.

Look within and find the readiness to share.
Remove from your shoulders the weight of guilt and
suffering.
Remove forever the curse of separation, of loneliness and
fear.
Take heed, My friends, and do this; do this now.

Know that My Love will support you.
My Law will guide you.
My Teaching will show you the future for all men, a
future bathed in the light of Living Truth.

Take Me to your hearts, My friends, and know Me as a
Brother.
Manifest That which I am and recreate the world.
Lift yourselves by My Love into the lap of God.

May the Divine Light and Love and Power of the One
Most Holy God be now manifest within your hearts and
minds.
May this manifestation lead you to see yourselves as My
warriors.

Message No. 118

February 10, 1981

My dear friends, it is with joy that I speak to you once more in this way and release to you some further facts of My Emergence.

My progress of Emergence continues well.
My plans are being fulfilled.
More and yet more of your brothers and sisters hear Me and respond well to My Call.
Knowingly or not they, too, await My Presence and to that fact respond.
They stand ready today to receive the means of change, the outlines of the New Dispensation for this world.
They stand ready to greet the dawn of that New Age which beckons all into divinity.

To make progress, man must die to the old.
Thus it ever was.
So, My friends, at this time of change must the old structures be renounced, and simply, in Brotherhood, must all men share.

Plans are afoot to bring Me closer to your eyes than before.
Likewise, steps have been taken to bring Me to the ears of many.
Thus do I set foot on My Mission's path.

When you see Me, My friends, you will see a Brother and Friend; you will see One Who knows the Way, long-since trodden.

My task is to take you with Me upon that simple Way and release in you your divinity.

When My Masters are known, They too will show you the steps on that Path.
They stand ready to emerge and to grasp the hands of men.
Make it your task, My friends, to make this known, and spread abroad the reality of My Coming.
Tell the world that Maitreya is here.
Tell them this, My brothers, and awaken in them, too, a sure hope for the future.
Good night, My dear friends.

May the Divine Light and Love and Power of the One Most Holy God be now manifest within your hearts and minds.
May this manifestation bring you joyfully running to My side.

Message No. 119

February 19, 1981

My dear friends, I am with you once again and am happy
to be so.

My plans unfold.
My Love grips the hearts of mankind, and slowly but
surely men turn to the Light.
All will be well; this I promise.
My Presence indicates the true future for man, for without
My Love man would go sadly astray.
My methods meet with success, however, and there is
naught to fear.

Presently, you will see Me in a new guise, presenting to
men the choices before them, outlining for you the
possibilities for the future, releasing to you the Laws of
God.
These Laws, My friends, enfold your lives.
Without the Plan of God, man is as naught.
Remember this always and restore balance.
Have within you always the sense of man's greatness,
man's oneness with all things, and man's divine scope.
Nevertheless, by himself man can do little.
Realise this and embrace the True Path.

My plans are formed in such a way that soon you will
know that the Teacher for the Age has come.
The Laws of God shall be fulfilled, and all shall be made
new.

Look for Me then as your Brother and Friend.
Seek Me in the midst of your brothers.
Know Me for My Love.
Recognise Me by My work.
See in Me the God you are.

My need is great for those who will work to make known
My Presence.
Take upon yourselves this task and lead the way.
Soon, My friends, all will know that the Anointed One is
here.
Why wait when you may stand in the vanguard?
My friends, there is nothing higher that you could do.
Make known My Presence, and abide always in My Love.
Make known My Presence, and see the future unfold.
Reveal to men that Maitreya is among them, and stand at
My side.
Good night, My dear friends.

May the Divine Light and Love and Power of the One
Most Holy God be now manifest within your hearts and
minds.
May this manifestation lead you swiftly to become My
heralds.

Message No. 120

February 26, 1981

My dear friends, I am with you once again, and with joy do I see the light of Aspiration around you.
This confirms for Me My knowledge of your readiness to work for Me.
My heart gladdens at the sight of this inner truth shining from the chalice of your heart.
Make way, My friends, for that Truth in your lives and open before you the door to the future.
My task is to illumine the path to that glorious future for mankind; to awaken in you the principle of Love; to lead you forward in manifesting that Love, each to the other, and thus draw all men to God.

I am the Savior returned.
I am a Man among men.
I am Hope embodied.
I am the Restorer of God's Law.
I am the Means to Knowing.

I bring succour to all men.
I love My brothers.
I count all men as One.
I teach the Law of God.
I combine Two Paths.
I seek to serve the world.
I love Justice.

I come in time.
I redress the balance of the world.
I commit Myself to the task.
I adore Liberty.

I sense the readiness of men.
I leave naught to chance.
I invoke the New.
I remedy past ills.
I transform the Old.
I touch your brow.
I command a host of angels.
I serve the Plan of God.
I embrace My brothers.

Enter with Me into the New Dawn and make all things
new.
Reveal That which I am through you and do My Work.
Express That which you are and create a New World.
Let My manifestation reveal yourselves as Gods.

May the Divine Light and Love and Power of the One
Most Holy God be now manifest within your hearts and
minds.
May this manifestation clear from your eyes the mists of
ignorance.

Message No. 121

March 3, 1981

My friends, I am with you once more.

Heavy, now, are My duties, but gladly, with joy, do I
return to the world.
My work may be lightened with your help.
I place before you now the opportunity to work thus for
Me, and to tell the world that I am here.
Make this known, My friends, on a world-wide scale, and
fashion a network of Hope which will sustain the world.

My Mission proceeds well and to plan.
All goes forward lawfully and in due time.
My face and My words are becoming more known to
your brothers, and soon all men shall know of My
Presence.
When I reveal My true identity and status, I shall appeal
to the heart's love of men to remake this anguished
world; to remove the fear of many; to restore the
birthright of millions of your brothers; to reawaken in
your hearts the Love of God.

Newly returned, I have but begun My Mission.
When the steps which I envision have been taken, My
true Teaching will begin.
Then shall I release to you the knowledge of your divine
heritage, awaken in you a new perception of Truth, kindle
in your hearts the Love of God, and reveal to you the
Laws of God.

Take upon yourselves a portion of My burden, and help
Me to restore the needed balance.
Take upon yourselves the task of succour and show
yourselves as My servants.
Hold before you the vision of the future which I embody,
and mount the ladder to God.

Be prepared to see Me soon.
Be ready to work with Me.

May the Divine Light and Love and Power of the One
Most Holy God be now manifest within your hearts and
minds.
May this manifestation lead you to see clearly My
Presence in the world.

Message No. 122

My dear friends, I am happy indeed to be among you once again in this fashion.

Likewise, I am happy to see the light of Aspiration which, as ever, surrounds the dedicated ones.
My need for such is great today.
Never in the history of this world has man stood in greater need of those who love their brothers, who love them and wish, above all, to serve them.
That flame of Service and Love, believe Me, burns brightly in the hearts of many today.
For that reason alone, I may say in full confidence that My Mission shall triumph.

Great, yet, is the work to be done.
Many are the obstacles to be set aside, but daily grow the hosts of Light, and on these, My people, I know I can rely.

My Emergence takes place under Law.
Many new avenues of approach are opening before Me.
Very soon now, in full and visible fact, shall you know that I am among you.
When will you add your weight to the wheel, My friends, My brothers and sisters?
Each one counts, however small and frail.
Spread abroad the fact that I am here, and bring to your work the force of My Love.

Let Me work through you and by you in creating the pool of Hope which will uplift and sustain this world.
Together let us work, My friends.

Together let us remake the old in the glowing raiments of the new.
Make way for My Love in your hearts and claim your birthright.

Many there are who know that I am here, but for many more by far that Blessing remains a forlorn hope.
Teach them the truth, My friends.
Make known your belief that Maitreya stands among you, walks the Earth once more, creates within you and through you the manifestation of your essential divinity.
Make this known, My friends, and become the Gods you are.
Make this known, My brothers, and inherit the Earth.
Make known your belief that I am here, and walk with Me into the sunlight of the New Time.
Create with Me that glorious future for all men.
Understand with me the nature of God and man.
My friends, I rely on you.
Know truly that time is short.

May the Divine Light and Love and Power of the One Most Holy God be now manifest within your hearts and minds.
May this manifestation quicken your stride and lead you to God.

Message No. 123

April 23, 1981

My dear friends, I am happy indeed to be with you once again in this way.

My plans proceed with success.
My hopes are being fulfilled.
My Emergence under Law takes place, and all is well.

The crime of separation, of division, of lawlessness must go from the world.
All that hinders the manifestation of man's divinity must be driven from our planet.
My Law will take the place of separation.
My Law is the Law of Love, of Brotherhood, of Justice and Truth.
Know these things and follow Me.
My Law will succeed, for the Law of Love emerges from the Being of God, and thus cannot fail.

While I am with you, I shall show you wonders of which you cannot dream.
I shall show you the nature of God in a new way.
I shall remove from your hearts the fear of death, the fear of life itself, the fear of your brother and yourself.
I shall help you to put behind you that ignorance, and to walk with Me in the new Light.

I seek your help for these tasks, My brothers, for naught of worth comes to man but through his own efforts.
Thus has it always been.

Take My hand, My friends, and I shall take you to a New
Country in which your true nature as Gods shall flourish,
in which all men together, as brothers, shall work out
their dream of life.

Many await My Coming with some fear.
Nothing but good shall grow where I tread.
My Promise stands:
I shall reveal to you the nature of yourselves and God.
I shall show you that for all men life is blessed.
I shall create among you a pool of Love from whose
waters all may quench their thirst.
My heart shall speak for your heart, My tongue for yours.
The leaders and the people will respond, and all shall be
made anew.

Take heart, My friends, I am here among you.
I come to serve you, to live with you and love you, to
lead you and guide you.
Look no more to the dark.
My Blessings go with you all.

May the Divine Light and Love and Power of the One
Most Holy God be now manifest within your hearts and
minds.
May this manifestation bring you nearer to your true
nature as Gods.

Message No. 124

April 30, 1981

My dear friends, it is with pleasure that I come among you once again in this way.

I come to tell you that all proceeds to plan.
My Emergence is following a certain rhythm and is well conceived.
By this means I enter quietly into your lives as One of yourselves.
Thus shall you know Me as a Brother, a Friend and Guide of you all.
My Masters, too, take Their places among you and share My burden.
I offer you the opportunity to help Them and Me, to share a little of the weight which I now carry for you.
Make known, My friends, your readiness to share, and lead the way into the future.

May it be that you shall see Me soon, and when you do, know that My heart beats with yours, My Love enfolds you always, My Will supports you, My Shield protects you.
Know this, then, and fear not.

Those who love their brothers are My people.
Those who stand on the threshold of the future are of My choice.
Those who know the way are My pupils.

Show the world, My dear ones, how well you are taught.

Show the world, My friends, that you stand for Justice and Love, for Sharing and Freedom, and manifest My Law.
I ask you to do this knowing you are here for this purpose.
I ask you to do this knowing you will not fail Me.

I shall place Myself before you as the Teacher of a new way for man, as the Leader out of the impasse, the quagmire of distrust and hate.
As the Revealer of the new Truths I am among you.
As the Dispeller of the old fogs of ignorance am I here.

Wait not a moment longer, but act, My friends and brothers.
My Blessings go with you all.

May the Divine Light and Love and Power of the One Most Holy God be now manifest within your hearts and minds.
May this manifestation reveal to you the truth of your presence on Earth.

Message No. 125

June 11, 1981

My dear friends, it is with great pleasure that I come among you once more in this fashion.

My planned Emergence proceeds.
Carefully, under Law, do I show My face.
Naught obstructs this progress but the creation of a pool of Hope, an air of expectation.
Create this, My friends, and help My Cause.
Make known the fact of My Presence to all who will listen, and welcome the New Time.
Confirm for yourselves the reality of My Return among you and begin the building of the New World.
I invite you to share with Me in this vital task and to enter into the Higher Service.

Many among you are afraid to speak.
Many hope that My Presence may indeed be true but fear the laughter of their brothers.
My friends, your brothers need the hope that this message brings, to lift them once again into the Lighted Way.
Spare not your efforts on My behalf, and share with your brothers that which you believe.
No higher work can you do for Me.

My Masters are entering the world One by One.
Soon you will see the results of Their work.

A new spirit of Hope is entering the Earth; to this all men will respond.

Fear not, My friends, for the Way is known, the Path for Us is old, the result is sure.
My Teaching will bring to you a new but simple Truth, and show you to yourselves as God.
My Teaching will release in you that Godhead, and further, thus, God's Plan.

Many await My Coming with trepidation, fearing the loss of all that they have loved, all that they have amassed and gained.
Fear not, My friends, for the loss will be the loss of separation only, of division and fear, of envy and hate.
To clear these from the world, all must be remade.
Know this, My friends, and be ready to share, to see your brother as yourself, to clasp him in your arms and call him friend.
In this way, My brothers, you manifest God's Plan.
Towards the completion of that Plan do I work and call you to My side.
Work with Me, My friends; together we shall make all things new.
Good night, My dear friends.

May the Divine Light and Love and Power of the One Most Holy God be now manifest within your hearts and minds.
May this manifestation lead you to see your brother as yourself.

Message No. 126

June 17, 1981

My dear friends, I am happy to be among you once again in this way.

I am happy, too, to tell you that My plans proceed well, with excellent results.
My Mission is to show you the Way to God, to unfold for you the simple Path to your Source.
I realise that for many that Path seems endless and fraught with difficulty.
Truly, My friends, this is not so.
We ourselves condition the Path as we enter in it.
When we are the Path, the Way opens before us, under Law.
Simple indeed is the Path to God.
Simple indeed are the steps thereon, and many are the helpers and guides on the Sacred Way.

My plans involve each one of you.
All have a place within the Plan of God.
When you know this, you will see that the Plan of God is the essence of your lives and supports and informs all Being, for the Plan of God is the nature of God Itself.

You, My friends, are no wise different from God.
Bring that divinity into manifestation and become the Gods you are.

Where, then, are the obstacles?
These, My friends, are man-made: the denial of the Law, the separation of man from man, child from loving child.
When men see this, the world will breathe and glow anew.

254

Make it your task, then, to teach the Law of Sharing, of Justice and Truth.

Help men to realise that without Justice and manifested Love, all else is as naught.

Mankind stands on the threshold of this discovery of Truth.

My Presence among you guarantees that this is so.

Help Me, My brothers and sisters, in My Task, and inform all you know that the need for Justice is paramount in our lives.

The lack of this alone separates man from man and threatens mankind itself.

Know this, My friends and brothers, and know that the Light will triumph.

Await My Teaching with expectation and trust.

Know that I am here and working for you.

Tell your brothers this.

Tell them that Maitreya, the Lord of Love, is among them; that the Teacher for the Age has come;

that the New World descends;

that the New Light beckons;

that men's hearts are open and ready for Truth.

Tell them this, My friends, and prepare My way.

May the Divine Light and Love and Power of the One Most Holy God be now manifest within your hearts and minds.

May this manifestation bring you to realise your place and worthiness in the Great Plan.

Message No. 127

July 1, 1981

My dear friends, I am happy indeed to be among you once again in this fashion.

My proposals inspire mankind.
Wherever you look throughout the world, the response to My Message can be seen.
The principle of Sharing, basic to men's lives, engages the minds of the leaders.
A growing group of such awakened men sound the keynote of the New Time.
Thus gladly do I see the response to My work.

My friends, you too can manifest Sharing in your lives; by all means should this divine principle govern.
Teach Sharing to your children, to the little ones, and enable them to cultivate the Good.
My task is to enlighten all men; to change ignorance into true knowledge and faith; to teach men that behind all that they see stands the One Reality, and thus to take them to God.

My plan is to include you, My friends, in My work, for to each is given a task to fulfil.
Know, My friends, that your task now is to share the burden of preparation for Me, to take upon yourselves a small part of the work, and make known My Presence to the world.

Each one inwardly knows this, knows that I am here, for each one has invoked Me, inwardly loves Me and, knowingly or not, seeks Me.

Is this not true, My brothers?

My standards are high, but then, so is the reward.
The goal is nothing less than complete identification with
God.
Achieve that, My friends, and know the meaning of Life.
My task is to teach you the simple path to that goal, to
take you step by step along the Golden Way, to place
before your feet the required Precepts and Truths, and to
steady you thereon.
My Masters, too, will guide you along the Way and serve
you as brothers.

My friends, time is short indeed when you will see My
face.
Take courage from this fact and announce to the world
that the Lord of Love is here, Maitreya Himself is among
you, the Teacher of the New has come.
Let all men know this, and raise them from despair.

My thanks for deeds done and My Love, as always, flow
to you all.

May the Divine Light and Love and Power of the One
Most Holy God be now manifest within your hearts and
minds.
May this manifestation lead you to accept Me as your
Brother, Friend and Guide.

Message No. 128

September 3, 1981

My dear friends, I am happy indeed to be among you once more in this fashion.

I may tell you that all goes well, all proceeds to plan.
This being so, daily My face becomes known more fully to your brothers.
Soon, for yourselves, you will see Me and, hopefully, accept My lead.

My plan is to continue My service in the shade for a little while longer.
By this means, mankind can declare its acceptance of Truth, of the New Light which shines from its heart.
Many today realise that the way to the future is through a new and just order, a new Brotherhood of man, a new spirit of co-operation between old enemies.
All this is possible today and is being effected.

A new light, My Light, shines over the Earth, and in its dazzle many stand amazed.
Working for Truth, for the benefit of all, they stand in awe of their power.
Likewise, My friends, within you all is the power of Truth.

Take your stand for Justice, Freedom and Life, and become equipped with the Power of God.
Naught can withstand the Power of God.
Naught can halt the Plan of God.
Naught, but for a time, can obstruct the Will of Divine God.

Know this to be true.
Remember this, My friends, and work as never before.

May it be that you will see Me soon.
When you do, My friends, know that your Brother is
among you, your Teacher has returned, your Guide into
the New Time is here.

Look for Me in the dark places, where hunger and strife
abound.
Know Me as the Brother of the poor, the rejected of the
world.
See Me thus, My friends and brothers, and see the Lord
of Love.

May the Divine Light and Love and Power of the One
Most Holy God be now manifest within your hearts and
minds.
May this manifestation lead you to the doors of the
oppressed.

Message No. 129

September 8, 1981

My dear friends, once again I am happy to be with you in this fashion.

My friends, I am glad indeed with the response of mankind.
Many see around them a world chaotic and dangerous, and rightly so.
Nevertheless, within the maelstrom of this apparent chaos is a still centre of calm, generating hope and change.
My friends, were you to see as I do the changes now occurring, your hearts would leap gladly as does mine, for throughout the world today man is awakening to change, bringing to the fore the new thoughts and ideals which now grip men's hearts.

Many of you are aware that much of good takes place in the world, yet hidden from you still are profound effects of My work.
Be therefore joyful and glad indeed.
Spread widely the rhythm and light of Joy and awaken in all you meet response to these glad tidings.
My friends, much remains to be done.
Much of weight engages My attention.
Many are the problems awaiting solution.
Nevertheless, great are the strides already made.
Know this to be true and act accordingly.

When you see Me, you will hear anew the old Truths.
From Me will come the enunciation of the true relationship of man to God.

Knowing this, those who respond shall go forward into that divinity.

Make it your task to teach the others.
Tell them what you know of Love and Truth.
Tell them that the manifestation of Love is the sure path to God.
This simple truth underlies all I teach.

Wait for Me a little longer.
See Me as your Brother and Friend.
Know Me as your Guide and hope for the future.
Trust Me and love Me as a Brother.
Know Me as the manifestation of the Love of God.
Prepare to see Me soon.
Prepare to work with Me.
Prepare to tell the world that you believe that I, Maitreya Himself, am now among you.
Do this for Me, My friends, and enter into Life.

May the Divine Light and Love and Power of the One Most Holy God be now manifest within your hearts and minds.
May this manifestation lead you to help the needy of the world.

Message No. 130

October 20, 1981

My dear friends, I am happy indeed to be with you once again in this fashion.

All goes well, augurs well for the future.
My plans proceed apace and galvanise mankind.
Wherever you may look in the world today, you will find change.
From top to bottom, the fabric of the old and decaying order is rent.
From this can we derive much satisfaction, for despite the pain involved in this process, a new and better world emerges.
Therefore, My friends, take comfort from this fact and look to the future with hope.

Many around Me now have recognised Me, work with Me and channel My Force.
Thus quietly do I work, remaking the world.
Help them and Me, My friends, and, too, gather around Me, lifting your brothers and sisters into Light, holding before them hope for the future.

My plans shall not fail.
My Emergence takes place.
My Gifts shall I bestow.
My words shall guide.
My Will shall strengthen.
My Teaching shall show you the nature of God.

I am God's Lieutenant.
I am man's Elder Brother.
I am the Source of Love.
I am the New.
I embody all that is best of the past.
I shall explain anew the nature of God and man.
I shall teach you to love.
I shall be among you.
I am with you always.
My heart beats in time with yours.

My preparations are well made.
My servers are ready.
My Truth kindles a new Light in men.
My Aim is sure.
My Spirit is blithe.
My Masters work with Joy.
My Guidance is yours to ask.

Take My hand, My friends, and let Me lead you over the river.
Let Me guide you over the narrow bridge.
Let Me show you the beauty which rests on the other side.
That beauty, My friends, is your true Self.
Help Me, My friends, to help you, and together let us transform this world.

May the Divine Light and Love and Power of the One Most Holy God be now manifest within your hearts and minds.
May this manifestation lead you to see yourselves as My advance guards.

Message No. 131

November 25, 1981

My dear friends, it is indeed a pleasure to be among you once more in this fashion, and to tell you of the progress of My Emergence.

In the days ahead, you will see Me as I am.
Look for Me, My friends, as a simple Man among men, recording for this time the hopes and fears of men.
I come to show you, My friends, that the age of cleavage ends, the time of division is passing.
From now, My friends and brothers, you will witness a leavening of the climate of the world: a sweeter atmosphere of hope will enter the affairs of men, a new call for Justice will sound forth from all quarters, and in the midst of that clamour will you find Me.

I shall sustain all who call for Peace, for Justice and brotherly Love.
I shall call to My side all who love their brothers.
From all parties and all nations they will come, gathering around Me.
I shall fill their hearts with hope and Love, and in mounting numbers they shall conquer the world.
This process has begun.
Already the voices of the people are being heard.
Louder and louder they cry for Justice, for Peace for all time.
A renewed hope seizes mankind, and this gladdens My heart.

You will see Me so soon now that, for the present, there is but one action to undertake.

Make known, with all the power of will and mind, My Presence in the world.

Make known, My friends, that you believe that the Son of Man walks again, that the Conveyor of God's Law is among you, that the Light of Truth beckons anew the hearts of men, that the transition into the New Age shall be, by far, smoother than supposed, that My Law shall flourish, that My Emergence is under way.

Tell your brothers, My friends, these truths, and bring them into your joy.

Look for Me soon, My friends, listen for My words, remember My Promise: I shall take all who are ready before the Throne of God.

My Blessings go with you all.

May the Divine Light and Love and Power of the One Most Holy God be now manifest within your hearts and minds.

May this manifestation lead you to stand firmly at your Brother's side.

Message No. 132

December 10, 1981

Good evening, My dear friends. I am happy to be among you once again in this fashion.

My message tonight is to encourage you in your belief in My Presence among you.
Verily it is so.
From My Descent until now I have lived as One of yourselves, a Man among men, known to your brothers as a Brother and Friend, known to them as a Counsellor and Guide, as their Leader and Spokesman.
Thus I am, and thus do I emerge into the world.
Look for Me thus, My friends, My brothers and sisters, and know that once again the Lord of Love walks the Earth.

My intention is to show you the simple path to the future, a path which will lead you directly to God.
Take My hand, My friends, and let us together walk that Path and know the meaning of Life, know the blessing of Love, know the purpose of God.

I am the Avatar of this coming Age.
I am the Messenger sent to show you the way.
I am the Tireless One, the Knower of Truth.
I am called by all men.
I am awaiting the hour of Emergence, that all may see Me.

I call on you, My friends, to make this so.
Make known that I am in the world.

266

Tell your brothers this truth and create among you a climate of hope.

Do this, My friends, My brothers and sisters, and know the meaning of service to the world.

Do this for Me, My friends, and raise the hope of your brothers.

Do this for the world, My brothers, and save the world.

My task is clear.

Yours is to respond.

I know already the choice of men.

May you be ready when you see My face.

My Blessings go with you all.

May the Divine Light and Love and Power of the One Most Holy God be now manifest within your hearts and minds.

May this manifestation lead you to realise your true worth at this time.

Message No. 133

December 16, 1981

Good evening, My dear friends. I am happy to be with you once again.

I see above and around you your aspiration for Truth.
My heart gladdens at this sight.
I shall take you, My friends, into a sphere of knowledge and Truth in which your very Godhead shall be realised.
Come with Me, My friends, awaken to your potential and know the joy of being God.

The answers to your problems are simple indeed.
Many times have I told you that the will to share must govern your lives.
Once again, I repeat: without Sharing and Justice, My brothers and sisters, man will know no peace.
Heed, then, My advice.
Take, then, the only open course and trust in Sharing to relieve the agony of the world.
My Teaching, thus, is simple.
Know, then, the joys of Brotherhood.
The principle of Sharing will lead you thereto.
Commit yourselves to this cause and know the joy of Service.
Commit yourselves to this work and realise your potential.
Make known by all means your stand for Justice and Peace, and help your suffering brothers elsewhere in the world.
My Teaching will show you that behind all appearances stands That which we call Life.
There is naught else anywhere in Cosmos.

Hold forever within you this concept, and realise your connection with that Life.

My Masters are preparing Themselves for Their work.
In growing numbers They shall enter your life and teach.
With Them as Friends, Brothers and Teachers, how can you fail?
With Their Presence among you, how can you fear?
Know this, My friends, and look to the future with hope.

My task of succour is but beginning.
When completed, I shall survey My work and yours, and see that all is well fashioned.
My Blessings flow to you from My heart.

May the Divine Light and Love and Power of the One Most Holy God be now manifest within your hearts and minds.
May this manifestation prepare you to realise yourselves as God-men.

Message No. 134

December 29, 1981

My dear friends, it is with joy that I greet you in this way at this year's end.

Many await the new year with impatience.
Rightly so, for this coming year will bring gifts in abundance, joyful participation and celebration of God's Will.
The destined Date of Declaration draws near.
On that day, My friends, you will see your Brother revealed as the Messenger of God.
Never before in the long history of man has such an event taken place in this way.
May you be blessed to be with us on that day.

My Masters, your Teachers, accept the Call of Service and take up quietly Their posts.
The vanguard of These, My Brothers, is already among you.
Soon you will recognise Them for what They truly are.
Give Them your trust and let Them teach you the ways of God.

My face remains hidden to you, but My words are not unfamiliar to your minds.
Know them as the words of your Brother Who loves you, Who longs to serve you, Who greets you as a friend, Who will take you to the further shore.

Try to believe, My friends, that I am here.
Try to accept that your Brother of Old is among you, and take up the challenge I give to you.

Help Me and help your brothers to make known My Presence.
Take the simple step of trust and awaken to your true worth.

Many await Me in fear, knowing not the cause of their confusion.
My friends, where fear stands, trust may not.
Why, then, hold to fear?
My Presence is apparent all around you.
Awaken to that fact.
Open your eyes to the changes in your world, in your own heart, in the Light of Joy in your child's eye.
Know that I am with you in these ways, My friends, and help to save the world.

Your cries have been heard.
Your longings have reached My heart.
Your pain is mine.
My Treasure shall I bestow on you.

May the Divine Light and Love and Power of the One Most Holy God be now manifest within your hearts and minds.
May this manifestation lead you to see your true role in this coming time.

Message No. 135

February 2, 1982

My dear friends, I am happy indeed to be with you once more in this fashion.

My Emergence proceeds.
Quickly, now, I enter the world's arena.
Within the coming months all shall see My face, shall hear My words of Truth, shall gather around Me in spirit and follow My lead.
Wherefore, then, need you fear?

A condition for My Coming was that men should share.
This divine principle now engages the minds of many.
Already the leaders gather and seek to implement this principle.
My message of Hope enters the hearts of all and quickens their love of Truth.
My friends, I am here with you to show you the way to Peace, which is the way to God.
Simple Justice will take you there.
Know this and create around you Justice and Love.
Know this and be ready to respond to My lead.

My Teaching is, as ever, simple indeed.
Men must share or die.
Loath am I to say this, but such is the truth, and many today now see this.

Forming themselves into groups, men of goodwill will brandish aloft their hopes and dreams of Justice and Peace.
This clamour will light the torch of Truth among the nations, and at its centre shall I be found.

272

Make way in your hearts for My Truth.
Make way in your hearts for My Love.
Manifest that Love around you and know the meaning of
Life.
Create thus the forms which will henceforth allow you to
manifest as Gods.
Do this with joy, My friends, and enter your heritage.

May the Divine Light and Love and Power of the One
Most Holy God be now manifest within your hearts and
minds.
May this manifestation lead you to see each other as the
Gods you are.

Message No. 136

February 25, 1982

My dear friends, I am happy indeed to be with you once again in this way, and to tell you that My Emergence proceeds.
Likewise, that of My Brothers, the Masters of Wisdom, proceeds apace.
When you see Us you will know that the New Time, the New Age, has begun — the time of Sharing and Justice, of Love and Brotherhood, the time of the Law of God.

I am the Instructor of this New Time.
I am its Forerunner.
I shall release to you That which will take you quickly home.
I shall give you these instructions which will release in you your divine nature.
From My Brothers will flow a stream of creative fire which will light your lamps and carry you brightly to God.

My Masters know naught but Love and Joy.
Likewise, My friends, this will be your heritage.
Make haste to claim your rights, and know the Love and Joy of God.

My purpose tonight is to tell you that many among you soon shall see Me, shall know Me for what I am, shall know that the Lord of Love is once again among you, the Teacher of Old walks the Earth once more.

You will know this, My friends, and tell it to your brothers, preparing them too for the New Time.

When you see Me, fear not: I come not to scold but to teach.

There are those among you who await Me as a judge and fear My Coming.

Naught that I say shall disappoint you; naught that I do shall cause you fear.

Know, My friends, My brothers and sisters, that I am your Friend, your Brother of Old, re-treading the Path of Old.

Know that My Love is with you always.
Know that My Shield protects you.
Know that My Will upholds you.
Know this, My friends, and fear not.

Await My Emergence with hope.
Be ready to work as never before.
Teach your brothers the fact of My Presence and give them, too, the gift of Hope.

My Blessings flow to you all.

May the Divine Light and Love and Power of the One Most Holy God be now manifest within your hearts and minds.

May this manifestation lead you to await the future with hope.

Message No. 137

March 30, 1982

I am with you once more, My dear friends.

Hopefully, My face will soon be seen by many of you,
but, in any case, on the Day of Declaration the world will
know that I, Maitreya, Son of Man, now dwell among you.

I have come to show you the possibilities which, as sons
of God, lie before you.
My heart knows your response, teaches Me your choice,
and awakens great gladness.
My friends, My people are everywhere, preparing for the
New World.
Their task is great, their burden heavy, their opportunity
unknowable.
Many there are now who see the way forward, hold
before men the Light of Truth, teaching men to share and
love, to cherish and trust.
Many now are awake to these divine aspects, and call for
the restructuring of your world.
My Force is behind them.
My Love inspires them.
My Will guides them.
In this way, I lead you into the New.

When you see Me, you will know that I have been always
with you, never far from your awakened heart.
Know this and trust that in this coming time I shall never
leave you, shall be with you always, to the end of the Age.
The time is short indeed till God's day of triumph.
Believe this and work as one to tell the world that I am
among you.

Do this for Me, My friends, and know the true joy of service to your brothers.

I call on you to make known at this late date that I, the Lord of Love, now walk among you.

My friends, the time is short.

Many hands and many voices are needed to proclaim this truth.

I know already those on whom I may count.

A final effort, My friends, and all will be as I have promised.

May the Divine Light and Love and Power of the One Most Holy God be now manifest within your hearts and minds.

May this manifestation lead you to make best use of the little time ahead.

Message No. 138

April 29, 1982

I am with you once again, My dear friends.

I am here to tell you that My Appearance to the world is
nigh.
Soon, all the world will see Me, will know Me and call
Me Brother.
I am your Brother, indeed, and return as such to proclaim
the truth of God's Presence within you, to direct your
steps into the future, to release to you the Love and Will
of God.

I come simply, as your Elder Brother and Friend, the
Lover of mankind, the Teacher for all men.
As leader of My group of Masters am I among you.
As Son of Man shall I appear before you.
In the creation of the New Age shall I guide you.
In all these ways shall I help.

My heart is full as now I begin My Task, full of Love and
Joy in its accomplishment.
That task is to take you with Me back to God, to the
Source of your Being, and to show those who are ready
His shining face.
My friends, My arms are held towards you.
Take eagerly My Gifts.

Choose to walk with Me into the Light of the future, and
know the meaning of Joy, the treasure of Love.
Do this, My friends, and grow into Gods.

When you see Me, you will recognise a Friend from long past, One Who has taught you often before.
Many will come to know this, will recognize Me, and allow Me to enter their lives.
Take with you this Pledge:
I shall restore to you the Law of God;
I shall bring to you God's Love;
I shall release into the world the Waters of Life.
In this precious stream shall you grow into your birthright.

My friends, if you would help Me, do this: make known to all that I am among you and restore to your brothers hope for the future.

My Love flows ever to you all.

May the Divine Light and Love and Power of the One Most Holy God be now manifest within your hearts and minds.
May this manifestation lead you soon now to become My people.

Message No. 139

May 21, 1982

I am with you once more, My dear friends.

I come once again to tell you that the path to God is simple indeed.
My way, the Way of Love, plots the shortest route.
The Path of Return is the Path of Joy.
Know this joy and return to God.

My Message is simple.
Take within you That which I bestow.
Release it to your brothers in joy, and find yourselves in the lap of God.
No man knew God who did not share.
All Love and all Life rest in that divine aspect.
Sharing, My friends, is the cornerstone of your lives.
Build well the Temple thereon.

My Appearance before men is nigh.
Already My group is known.
Many are the avenues to My abode.
Knock gently therein, and I shall answer.
Certain of My Teachings have been revealed.
Much yet remains to be disclosed.
My desire is to open for you the treasure chest of My Wisdom, and to teach you all things pertaining to God.
Allow Me to do this.

Allow Me to share with you My Oneness with the Father, to reveal His nature to you, and to lead you to His feet.
My way, the simple Way of Love, will lead you into His arms.

My friends, there is much, much to know of the nature of God.

All but a tiny fragment so far remains hidden to you.

With My help you will come to know the glory of the Being in which you dwell, and of which you are a reflection.

Know this and work with Me.

Know this and allow Me to guide you.

See this and take gladly My hands, and accept your inheritance.

Many now await the sight of My face.

Soon, soon now, all men everywhere will know the truth of My Coming.

Maitreya, your Friend, your Brother of Old, is indeed among you.

Good night, My dear friends.

May the Divine Light and Love and Power of the One Most Holy God be now manifest within your hearts and minds.

May this manifestation lead you to accept quickly My Teaching.

Message No. 140

May 27, 1982

My dear friends, I am happy to be with you once again, and to give you this last communication in this way.

It has been My intention to reveal Myself at the earliest possible moment, to brook no delay, and to come before the world as your Friend and Teacher.
Much depends on My immediate discovery, for in this way can I help you to save your world.
I am here to aid and teach, to show you the path to the future, and to reveal you to each other as Gods.

I am sure you realise that much depends on the actions of men in the coming years.
All the world knows this.
All the world stands in fear.
Nevertheless, there is a growing sense of hope, a likelihood of change, a response to My Presence, creating thus a point of stillness in the tension.

Hopes now run high for My Appearance.
Gladly would I present Myself to the people.
Look for Me then, and find Me waiting.
Search for Me then, and grasp My hand.

I need your help to come before you, to bless this world and teach, to show men that the way forward is simple, requires only the acceptance of Justice and Freedom, Sharing and Love.
These aspects are already within you and need only to be evoked by Me.

Christ is here, My friends.
The Avatar has come.
Your Brother walks among you.
My Mission begins.
Know Me soon and help your brothers to know Me.
Take My hand and let Me lead you to God.

May the Divine Light and Love and Power of the One
Most Holy God be now manifest within your hearts and
minds.
May this manifestation lead you quickly to see your roles
in this heroic time.

FURTHER READING

Books by Benjamin Creme

The Reappearance of the Christ and the Masters of Wisdom

Creme's first book gives the background and pertinent information concerning the return of Maitreya, the Christ, including: the effect of the reappearance on the world's existing institutions, the anti-christ and forces of evil, the soul and reincarnation, meditation, telepathy, nuclear energy, UFOs and ancient civilizations, the problems of the developing world and a new economic order.

ISBN #0-936604-00-X, 256 pp

Maitreya's Mission — Vol. I

Offers much new information on the story of Maitreya's emergence and on such subjects as: the work and teachings of Maitreya, the externalization of the Masters of Wisdom, life ahead in the new age, evolution and initiation, meditation and service, healing and social transformation, the Seven Rays.

3rd Edition. ISBN #90-71484-08-4, 411 pp

Maitreya's Mission — Vol. II

A unique compilation on such subjects as meditation, growth of consciousness, political and economic change, psychology, health, the environment, initiation, group work, world service, and science and technology in the new age. Includes interviews with a Master of Wisdom, as well as the current teachings and forecasts of Maitreya, the World Teacher. Offers provocative explanations for such phenomena as crop circles, crosses of light, visions of the Madonna, healing waters and UFOs.

ISBN #90-71484-11-4, 718 pp

Maitreya's Mission — Vol. III

A chronicle of the next millennium. Political, economic and social structures that will guarantee the necessities of life for all people. New ways of thinking that will reveal the mysteries of the universe and release our divine potential—all guided and inspired by Maitreya and

the Masters of Wisdom. Includes a compilation of the ray structures and points of evolution of 950 initiates throughout history.
ISBN #90-71484-15-7, 704 pp

Transmission: A Meditation for the New Age

Describes a dynamic group process of stepping down powerful spiritual energies directed by the Masters of Wisdom. Introduced by Benjamin Creme, at the request of his own Master, this potent world service stimulates both planetary transformation and personal growth of the individuals participating.
4th Edition. ISBN #90-71484-17-3, 204 pp

A Master Speaks

Articles by Benjamin Creme's Master from the first 12 volumes of *Share International* magazine. The book includes such topics as: reason and intuition, health and healing, life in the new age, glamour, human rights, Maitreya's mission, the role of man.
2nd Edition. ISBN #90-71484-10-6, 256 pages

The Ageless Wisdom Teaching

This introduction to humanity's spiritual legacy covers the major principles: the Divine Plan, source of the teaching, evolution of human consciousness, the Spiritual Hierarchy, energies, the Seven Rays, karma, reincarnation, initiation, and more. Includes a glossary of esoteric terms.
ISBN #90-71484-13-0, 62 pp

❧

The above books have been translated and published in numerous languages. They are available from local bookstores and from various online vendors.

❧

Extensive information on this subject may also be found at:
www.ShareIntl.org

Share International

A UNIQUE MAGAZINE featuring each month: • up-to-date information about Maitreya, the World Teacher • an article from a Master of Wisdom • expansions of the esoteric teachings • articles by and interviews with people on the leading edge in every field of endeavor, including: the eradication of hunger and poverty; social and economic change; politics, peace and human rights; science and medicine; psychology and education • news from UN agencies and positive developments in the transformation of our world • Benjamin Creme's answers to a variety of topical questions submitted by subscribers and the public.

Share International brings together the two major directions of new age thinking — the political and the spiritual. It shows the synthesis underlying the political, social, economic and spiritual changes now occurring on a global scale, and seeks to stimulate practical action to rebuild our world along more just and compassionate lines.

Share International covers news, events and comments bearing on Maitreya's priorities: an adequate supply of the right food, adequate housing and shelter for all, healthcare and education as universal rights, the maintenance of ecological balance in the world.

Versions of *Share International* are available in Dutch, French, German, Japanese, Romanian and Spanish. For subscription information, contact the appropriate office below. [ISSN #0169-1341]

For North, Central and South America,
Australia, New Zealand and the Philippines
Share International
P.O. Box 971, North Hollywood, CA 91603 USA

For the UK
Share International
P.O. Box 3677, London NW5 1RU UK

For the rest of the world
Share International
P.O. Box 41877, 1009 DB Amsterdam, Holland